Enhance Your Masonic Knowledge

RONALD J. R. HART

Lewis Masonic

First Published 2013

ISBN 978 0 85318 430 0

Illustrations © Ronald Hart
Illustrations and Digital Enhancement – Rowan Lee-Foyster

Published by Lewis Masonic

an imprint of Ian Allan Publishing Ltd,
Hersham, Surrey KT12 4RG

British Library Cataloguing in Data
A catalogue record of this book is available from the British Library

Visit the Lewis Masonic website at www.lewismasonic.com

List of Illustrations & Credits
Map of the Gulf of Aqaba © *Rowan Lee-Foyster*
The Noble Orders of Architecture © *Ronald Hart*
Capitals of the Columns © *Ronald Hart*
The Architecture of the Arch © *Ronald Hart*
The Entrance to the Temple with the Two Pillars – Jachin and Boaz © *Ronald Hart*
The Temple Facing East © *Ronald Hart*
The Temple Facing West © *Ronald Hart*
Celestial and Terrestrial Globes © *Rowan Lee-Foyster*
Tracing Board Found at Pompeii, 1874 © *Rowan Lee-Foyster*
Ground Plan of Temple at Pompeii © *Ronald Hart*
Illustration of a Stone in Bath Museum 133BC © *Ronald Hart*
The Symbolism of the Past Master's Jewel © *Ronald Hart*
The Seal of Lodge Mother Kilwinning © *Ronald Hart*
Author's Impression of the Vaulted Chamber © *Ronald Hart*

CONTENTS

Chapter 1

Myth and Legend

That which is myth may be disproved; that which is legend may pass away; but that which is enshrined in ritual has exceeding permanence in the affairs of men. Thus both myth and legend themselves unreal – establish a vicarious reality for themselves in Masonic Ritual, and the study of myth and legend thereby begins to assume an ethical importance, which overflows its own boundaries of imagination into the practical realities of everyday life.

It may perhaps be a pardonable exaggeration, but nonetheless an exaggeration to say that Freemasonry is blended indestructibly with the rites, ceremonies and traditions of Hebrew worship. This is not entirely and literally true in all respects but, on the other hand, it is true that we do have in our Craft Lectures and in those of other associated Masonic Rites, numerous traditions respecting the building of King Solomon's Temple in which we find recited some of the architectural and ornamental details of the mighty edifice, and details of some of the personalities involved, from all of which we attempt to derive a suitable symbolism leading to an ethical and spiritual philosophy.

In some cases, our Masonic legends respecting King Solomon can in fact be found to be a reflection of the Rabbinic and Cabbalistic lore that had been current among the Jews from very early times, and among the Arabs as well, to whom 'Suleiman' (considered by them to have been a Muslim) is almost as fabulous a figure as he is to his own kinsmen and to Masonry. Both to the Jews and the Arabs, he is the Wise Man par excellence and Master Magician. Many are the tales told of his prowess and his wisdom, his miraculous domination of the 'demons and the jinns', his occult and superhuman powers and faculties. Of special interest to R. A. Masons is the Rabbinic legend to the effect that Solomon, in his capacity as prophet and seer foresaw the destruction of his Temple by the Babylonians, and accordingly had an underground room built below the Temple in which the Ark was eventually hidden. Our wise king Solomon – in his time Grand Master of Masonry and Architecture.

More recently found within the façade of the eleventh-century Würzburg Cathedral, were two pillars flanking a Gothic doorway leading to a small vaulted chamber, perhaps an allusion to Solomon's Porch or as a piece of Symbolism. Incidentally, the names of these two pillars were here found inscribed as I A C H I O N and BO O Z, each in two separated syllables.

Note: The now anglicised 'J' is universally represented in Hebrew by the sound 'Y' e.g. Jerusalem *Yerusha-layim*.

BOOZ: this could be the result of an incorrect use of the word in the early Masonic Catechisms. I quote from a 1711 Catechism, the *Trinity College Dublin*

MS, where it is stated: 'The Enterprentices sign is *sinues*, the word is *Boaz* its hollow.' This appears to be a mistaken reference to the left-hand Solomonic Pillar, but only through a misunderstanding on the part of the writer of the MS, who evidently thought that the word BOAZ had something to do with the now obsolete and like-sounding word 'bose' or 'boss' and which does, or did at one time, mean hollow. This is correctly indicated in another catechism – *A Mason's Confession*, 1721 – which curiously states, "If I should come to a Mason working at stone, and say, 'That stone lies boss', the Prentice is taught to answer; 'It is not so boss but it may be filled up again', or 'It is not so boss as your head would be if your (hams) brains were out.'"

Another catechism *Sloane MS No3329* of the year 1700 states: 'If he takes one of their tools or his own staff and strikes softly on the wall or work, saying "This is boss or hollow", the Prentice will answer, 'It is solid.' Architecturally and Masonically, the most important feature of King Solomon's Temple was without doubt the pair of pillars in the Porch. The amount of space devoted to a detailed description of these pillars in the Bible is also a fair indication of their previous religious importance. This habit of moralising the names of these two pillars is not a Masonic invention. These Pillars were set up to note that it was God that gave him the power and dominion over all these Nations, and had fulfilled his promise made to Moses and to his people Israel.

The tops of the pillars were curiously adorned, to show that those who persist to the last constantly should be crowned. The lily work symbolised the emblem of innocence; pomegranates of fruitfulness, these being many grains in one apple, their Crown shall declare their glory.

It was the custom among the ancient Hebrews of giving significant names to sacred objects. Modern Biblical scholars are generally agreed that the names of these two pillars must be enigmatical.

Furthermore, they must have a religious significance: the pillars have names because they are sacred objects. Similarly, the Babylonians had this custom of bestowing significant and sacred names upon buildings (See *Exodus 17:15*.) In celebration of the Israelites' victory over the Amalekites, Moses built an altar and called the name *Adonai-nissi* (The Lord is my Banner). Thus we establish the fact that the two pillars were not merely articles of Architectural adornment or function, but must have been sacred objects.

These pillars are believed by some Masonic and non-Masonic writers to have been structural members, with an entablature supporting the roof, or as supporting a pair of traverse screens. Most commentators, however,-Lay, Clerical and Masonic – accept them to have been freestanding columns, purely ornamental or emblematic just as they are depicted on our Tracing Boards. These Pillars of Solomon may perhaps have been set up more specifically in imitation of the Obelisks that have been found at the gateways to Egyptian

Temples. For example, the Obelisks at the entrance of the Temple at Karnak are very impressive in this connection, or, perhaps they may have been copied from Tyre, the home of the workmen who wrought them, and where Heroditus, sometime later, reported to have seen two similar pillars standing before the Temple of Hercules, one of pure gold, and the other of emerald. Two such pillars were found at the entrance to the temple of Byblos later known as Gebal the home of the Giblites, the stone-squarers of King Solomon's Temple.

In Syria, excavations have uncovered the small Chapel of the eighth century Kings of that city; likewise two pillars were in the Porch of the Syrian Temple, standing free, purely ornamental or symbolical rather than architecturally functional. As to the Egyptian Obelisks, the best known is perhaps the pair that Tuthmosis III had erected at Heliopolis City of the Sun in the fifteenth century BC, which Augustus Caesar later removed to the *Caesareum* at Alexandria. One of these now adorns the Thames Embankment in London, the other is in Central Park, New York. Both are commonly referred to as 'Cleopatra's Needle'.

But why *two* pillars, if but *one* deity is thus represented? Among the Semites and other primitive peoples, Gods went in pairs! Male and Female as Baal and Ashtoreth; Osiris and Isis, and so on. Possibly the two pillars stood for Male and Female, the active and passive principle in nature.

The pillars are said to have been cast in the plain of Jordan, in the clay ground between Succoth and Zeredatha (*II Chronicles 4:17*) along with all the other vessels and utensils of brass. These localities Succoth and Zeredatha are on either side of the River Jordan, Succoth on the east bank about a mile north of the River Jabbok (*See map*). To date, no archaeological remains of a Solomonic Foundry have been uncovered in this region. But in 1938, the discovery occurred of smelting and working metals of King Solomon's era, in the form of deposits of copper ore in areas south of the Dead Sea, which appear to have been worked with particular intensity. This discovery is of even greater importance than that of the Stables, because of its direct connection with Solomon's Temple activity. Here, in fact, we find the source of the raw materials for Solomon's two brass pillars, his enormous Brazen Sea that stood before the Temple, the brass Altar, the elaborate ten brass bases, and ten lavers of brass, the pots, shovels and basons, all the vessels which Hiram made KS for the house of the Lord (*Kings 7.*)

Note that it is considered that the *brass* and *bronze* in our English Bibles is a mistranslation of the original. It should read *copper* instead, since brass and bronze were not known in ancient times.

The discovery at Ezion-geber at the tip of the Gulf of Aqaba presents a site of curious location, open to the full fury of the winds and sand-storms blowing in from the north as if forced through a wind tunnel, at the cost of much inconvenience and discomfort for its inhabitants, but it is an ideal site

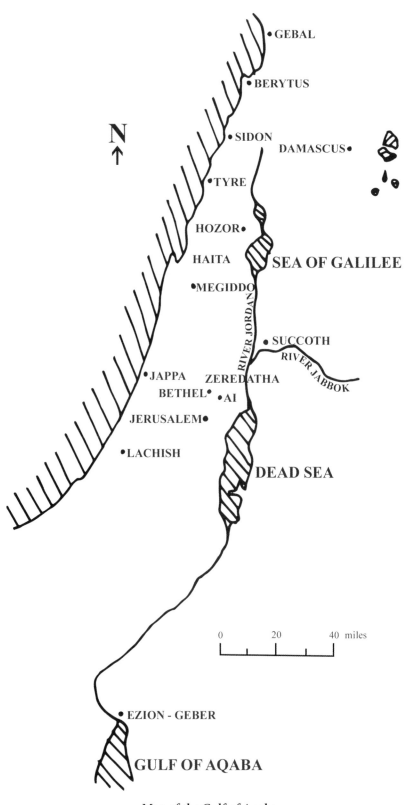

Map of the Gulf of Aqaba

for that very reason for a natural smelter refinery; a nature-and-man-made Bessemer Furnace, in fact, with the fierce, natural winds taking the place of artificially compressed air in the man-made structure excavated on this site. The construction too, was found to be as curious as its location, the walls being found pierced with two rows of flues, and interconnected by a system of air channels, to take advantage of the prevailing windstorms. It was evident that the building was an elaborate smelter or refinery, where previously roasted ores were worked into ingots of pure metal, devoted mainly to copper and in a lesser degree to iron. Ezion-geber was the Pittsburgh of Palestine.

The pottery whereby the stratum of the site was dated belongs to the time of King Solomon. It must have taken a great deal of business ability as well as Architectural, Engineering and Metallurgical skill on the part of the developers of this Solomonic venture. To construct the factory town and seaport of Ezion-geber, as well as keeping the production line going, bricks had to be made by the thousands and laid by expert masons as soon as they were manufactured. Some of the walls of the smelter have stood to almost their original height for nearly thirty centuries. Thousands of labourers had to be assembled, housed, fed and protected at the site. Skilled technicians of all kinds had to be recruited, and great caravans were organised to transport food and materials. An effective business organisation had to be convened to regulate the profitable flow of raw materials, and finished and semi-finished products. Only one man possessed the strength, wealth and wisdom capable of initiating and carrying out such a highly complex and specialised undertaking. He was King Solomon, that wisest mere man, the Prince of Peace and Architecture, the Grand Master Mason of his day.

Ezion-geber represents one of his greatest, albeit up to the present time, his least known accomplishments. We learn from the Bible that Solomon had a port on the Red Sea at precisely this point, hereby borne out by the excavation at Ezion-geber, disclosing such objects as copper, iron nails, rope and tar. Jewish commentators regard it as an historical fact that the town of Gebal contained a Guild of Stone Masons; the neighbourhood was a rocky one and afforded opportunities for the locals to become expert in the hewing and dressing of stone. *I Kings 5:18* indicates that as the builders of Solomon and Hiram of Tyre did the woodwork for the Temple, so the Giblites did the stonework; hence the explanatory translation of *Giblin* as stone-squarers.

If you make a mistake in arithmetic or composition, you can correct it or even tear it up. If a picture or a statue is ugly, it can be put out of sight or destroyed, but if a building is ugly or out of true, there it stands for all time for all to view. Its ugliness or its mistakes cannot be covered up or corrected. This once caused so much concern to an architect that he committed suicide. Just as the great temple he had planned and designed was completed, he left a note stating he had made five mistakes in the building and since they could not be covered up or corrected, they were there for all time and the disgrace he could never live with. Most buildings have many mistakes; some are ugly, though few people ever notice anything wrong.

But there was a building erected over two thousand years ago that had no mistakes. It is one of the very few perfect buildings in the world, and was built for a woman in honour of a Greek Goddess, the Goddess of Wisdom, whose name was *Athene Parthenos*, the building being called after her last name, the Parthenon. The Egyptians built their temples with the columns on the inside. The Greek temples had the columns on the outside; their temples were not to hold people but to house the statue of their God. People did not go inside to worship as we do today but stood on the outside. The columns used by the Greeks were simpler and much more beautiful than those of the Egyptians. Greek Temples had three types of columns; the one used in the Parthenon was the Doric column – the 'man's style of column'. It is called Doric after a very old Greek Tribe. Not only the columns but also the style of building that went with *it* was strong, simple and plain; that is why it is called 'man's style.'

Styles in ladies' fashions change often, but the Doric style of building has lasted over two thousand years. The Doric Column has no base, but rests directly on the Platform. It also tapers slightly, just as a tree trunk does. Its

GREEK DORIC	GREEK IONIC	GREEK CORINTHIAN	ROMAN DORIC	ROMAN IONIC	ROMAN CORINTHIAN
1	2	3	4	5	6

The Noble Orders of Architecture

sides are not perfectly straight, although they may appear to be so, for they bulge slightly. This bulge is known as 'entasis'. Columns were given entasis because columns with straight sides looked thin in the middle. Some of today's architects have thought to improve the Doric column by increasing the bulge, just as some people when the Doctor prescribes one pill, take two – reasoning that if one pill is good for you, two must be better but the Greek entasis was just exactly enough. Add more entasis and the column looks fat and ugly like a man who is fat around the middle.

The sides of the Doric column were then fluted, to create a slender shadow-line from top to bottom of the column. Most modern columns have no fluting. You can well imagine the difficulty of cutting such slender channels of perfection in marble. One slight mistake and the column is ruined.

Men have tried ever since the time of the Parthenon to improve on the Doric. It seems impossible to do so, since every change from the original is less beautiful. The Greeks had what we call a 'good eye' for the look of a building. It takes a 'good eye' to judge a building's proportions for defects. Some of us can't even judge if a picture hangs straight on a wall!

Two important tools used by the Operative Mason are the plumb line and level you are all fully aware of their Masonic uses and applications. The Greeks said you could not believe the plumb line and level. For instance, columns that are truly vertical appear to lean out, whilst floors that are really level or horizontal seem to sag in the middle try this as an exercise. This is because our eyes make them appear out of true, an optical illusion. We see buildings with our eyes and the Greek builders of the Parthenon constructed it as they wanted their eyes to see it; so although all lines may seem to be vertical, horizontal, level or straight, there is really not a vertical or a horizontal or a perfectly straight line in the Parthenon. That is one of the things that make the Parthenon so extraordinary. Its columns were not made of single blocks of stone, but of drum-shaped pieces that were cut with such exactitude, they fitted with such perfection that no joint showed. It is even said that the pieces have grown together like a broken bone that is well set Ionic masterpiece.

It may seem rather farfetched to say a building is like a woman, but the ancient Greeks had far-fetched imaginations. They imagined, for instance, that a vain boy had been turned into the flower we call the narcissus; that a girl who dared to love the beautiful sun god was turned into the sunflower; or that a nymph had been turned into a laurel tree. So it was not such a great stretch of the imagination, after all, for them to say that a woman had been turned into a certain kind of column or that a certain kind of marble column was like a woman.

An architect named Vitruvius, who lived a hundred years before Christ, said that the two curls on the head of this column were the locks of the woman's hair; that the grooves or flutings in the body of the column were the folds of her gown; and that the base of the column was her bare feet. They called this kind of column 'Ionic' because it was first made in Ionia, a colony of Greece across the sea in Asia Minor. The best Ionic building was the Erechtheum on the Acropolis, it was called the Erechtheum because it was built in honour of Erechtheus who was supposed to have been King of Athens in days long past. We have heard that the Parthenon was a man's style building built in honour of a woman. The Erechtheum was a woman's style building, built in honour of man. Ionic columns were on three sides of the Erechtheum, but on the fourth end there are six statues of full-sized women in place of columns, and they are supporting the roof on their heads. It is called the Porch of the Maidens. The story is that they represent captives from Carya, condemned to stand in this position, holding the roof on their heads forever.

Women today go to Paris for their dress styles; architects used to go to Greece for their styles in building. Some have tried to start new styles in columns, others just something new and different, but all have failed to equal the beauty and proportions of the previously mentioned columns. The Greeks did start a new style of column called the 'Corinthian,' but they did not like it very much and hardly ever used it. The old architect Vitruvius tells of another legend to explain the Corinthian capital. A basket of toys with a tile over the top was placed on the grave of a little girl in Corinth, as was the custom in those days. But by chance, the basket had been placed directly over a thistle

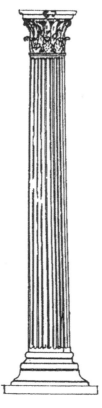

CAPITAL OF A COMPOSITE   CAPITAL OF A CORINTHIAN   CORINTHIAN COLUMN

Capitals of the Columns

plant and the leaves of the thistle grew up around the basket. An architect seeing this thought it would make a good design for a capital, so he copied it in marble and put it on an Ionic column in place of the Ionic capital, hence the invention of the Corinthian column which is just an Ionic column with a different capital. The Greek thistle is called the acanthus and the leaves that curl upwards and outwards of the capital are acanthus leaves. Just under the tile which is called the abacus, are four corner-scrolls or curls, like curl shavings a carpenter makes with his plane, but not like those of the Ionic capital which are like rolls of music. The Ionic curls face front and back; the Corinthian curls face corner-wise.

Many people think the Corinthian capital is more beautiful than either the Doric or the Ionic, but others think it too fancy and not natural to have stone beams resting upon leaves.

By the third century before Christ, all the finest Greek architecture was in existence. After that there was a gradual decline in all the arts, as the power of Greece shrank away and that of Rome spread.

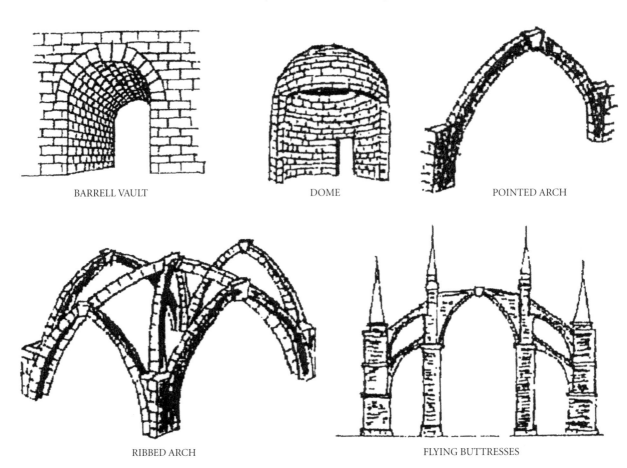

BARRELL VAULT   DOME   POINTED ARCH

RIBBED ARCH   FLYING BUTTRESSES

The Architecture of the Arch

The Greeks were great architects, but the Romans were great builders. There is a difference. The Romans built many fine buildings, but their taste wasn't as good as that of the Greeks. The Romans liked the Corinthian better than either the Doric or the Ionic: and they also made another column, composed of both the Ionic and Corinthian capitals. This column is called 'Composite'; it had the large curls of the Ionic and acanthus leaves of the Corinthian. Often it is hard to tell whether a column is Corinthian or Composite. In the Composite column, the Ionic top is larger than in the Corinthian.

The Romans also changed the Doric column; they gave it a base and left out the flutings and the saucer-shaped part of the capital. This kind of Roman column was called 'Etruscan Doric' or 'Tuscan'.

The Romans made other changes in their styles of building changes for the worse. In order to make columns seem higher than they were, they frequently put a box-like base or pedestal beneath each column. They placed split- or half-columns against walls. These are known as 'engaged'. Other columns they flattened out against the wall, so that they appeared square, and these are known as 'pilasters'.

The greatest thing the Romans did for building was the use of the arch. Assyrians invented the arch but hardly used it because very little stone was available with which to build arches. Moreover, they never rested their arches on columns. The Greeks and other architects before them placed a single stone across from column to column, known as 'post-and-lintel'. With this method, spans between columns were short, because a single slab of stone could not reach very far. The Romans were the first to make arches from column to column; they also made barrel vaults and domes, which were arched ceilings, built on the same principle as the arch. Discrepancies, or apparent discrepancies, with respect to the pillars, are to be noticed in the Biblical accounts. Also archaeological and architectural evidence is open to criticism with regard to their height, which is given as 18 cubits in *Kings* and 35 cubits in *Chronicles*. The length of a cubit in this instance is generally taken to be 1.5ft; but in fact there are a number of cubits used at different times for varying kinds of measurement. For example: 3 cubits equals 6ft, 'building cubit' equals 14.4ins. A 'royal cubit' was used in the building of the temple and this equals 20.9ins. The progress of archaeological investigation will make the Bible stand out more and more brightly against the background of the ancient orient, and I have no doubt that time and circumstance will restore the original.

I must point out that a history of Architecture is not a history of Freemasonry the latter is essentially the history of an organisation rather than the history of an art, despite the many points of contact between the two.

The Temple at Karnak (previously mentioned) partly built by Rameses the Great, is now in ruins and is considered one of the most beautiful ruins in the world. You may not accept this as beauty. A broken-down man or a dilapidated house is not usually beautiful; then why do you suppose this ruin of Karnak is called beautiful? The main columns, which supported its roof, were 70ft high, and these columns were made to look either like a single lotus flower or a bouquet of lotus flowers. Mere size does not make a thing beautiful, for a large building may be very ugly.

The pyramids, for instance, are monuments to man's attempt to construct something enduring, lasting. The builders succeeded in building the most permanent, lasting thing ever built by man. The pyramids were also monuments to their belief in a life after death. When we think of the millions of people who have come and gone, lived and died since these mighty monuments were built, and the still countless millions who will come and go while the pyramids still continue to stand, it surely must make us consider the shortness of our lives and the awesome length of eternity to which we might piously add 'So mote it be.'

Chapter 2

Origins of Our Lodge Columns

In the *Charge after Initiation*, the hope is expressed that Initiates will feel themselves called upon "to make a daily advance in Masonic knowledge". How seriously do you all observe this obligation? How many of you take such a deep interest in Freemasonry as you should and could? What effort do any of you make to learn more of the history and the principles of the Craft to obtain a deeper understanding of our beautiful ritual?

So it is with many who are admitted into Freemasonry. They only observe the forms, the ceremonies, the emblems and the jewels, and they hear the lectures and charges; but they fail to discern the ethics and philosophy thereof. They hear the enunciation that Freemasonry is a science of morality, veiled in allegory and illustrated by symbols but again fail to fathom its meaning and, consequently, do not solve the allegories nor discern the significance of the symbols.

Let me test your powers of observation. How many columns and pillars are there to a Lodge? Three; not five or seven as some believe. On which of the two columns should the terrestrial globe be fixed? Have any of you ever considered this?

We now have an opportunity to consider the origins of the columns by delving into our Masonic History and consulting the "Old Charges" of our Operative Brethren. These Charges were recorded on old manuscripts, of which there are many still available. However; we need only refer to the two earliest, the *Regius Manuscript*, dated 1390, and the *Cooke Manuscript*, dated 1425. These can be seen in the British Museum.

These two manuscripts have slight differences: but, in brief, they consist of a Prayer of Invocation; a historical section, opening with an account of the Seven Liberal Arts; the "Old Charges" themselves, which you are, no doubt, aware have been condensed and recorded in our *Book of Constitutions*.

A Biblical story of the Histories is told in the *Book of Genesis*, Chapter 4 verse 16 onwards. These recount how Lamech, the great grandson of Cain, had three sons and a daughter. The sons were named Jabal, Jubal and Tubal-cain; they, with their sister, Naamah, were the founders of all the Crafts in the world, and, according to legend about 1500 BC these four children of Lamech, fearing God would take vengeance for sin by destroying the world, either by fire or water, decided to inscribe the sciences they had founded upon two pillars; one made of marble, the other made of clay-brick, suggesting one would not burn and the other would not sink in water. In theory, they considered these two pillars would preserve the knowledge of mankind over an impending destruction which, as you all know, proved to be Noah's Flood.

The Entrance to the Temple with the Two Pillars – Jachin and Boaz

Legend recalls that after the flood, one pillar was found by Hermes the Greek god of science; the other by Pythagoras the Greek philosopher. After careful study, each proceeded to teach the knowledge they had derived from the inscriptions engraved upon the columns. These were the only two pillars referred to in the old Manuscript Charges of 1400 onwards. There are some 130 separate versions of them still extant, where King Solomon's Temple played only a very small part; and there is no mention of his two pillars at all.

The period of change from these original columns to those in which today's interest centres is a mystery which may never be solved, although pointers indicate that a gradual development in our modern ritual between the years 1450 – 1700 in which versions of both sets of columns were referred to in the same texts.

It is not until about AD 1700 that King Solomon's two pillars are named in our earliest ritual documents first by Biblical references and later with further expansions of strong Christian religious symbolism. In 1724 or 1725 two other exposures of the ritual state that the two Solomonic Pillars represent the strength and stability of the Church, in all ages.

I make it quite clear at this point that the two columns of marble and brick, referred to in the "Old Charges" as well as the two pillars at the porch of King Solomon's Temple are in no way connected with the Three Great Columns of Wisdom, Strength and Beauty that support our Lodge. The first mention of the latter was found in 1730 and was considered separate as well as being purely symbolical; and also, at that time, they were not a part of the Lodge furniture.

However, in 1760 it was recorded that the Wisdom column represented the Master in the East; the Strength column represented the Senior Warden in the West; and the Beauty column represented the Junior Warden in the South (The Doric, the SW; the Ionic, the WM; and the Corinthian, the JW.) This implies that these three columns were now something more than verbal symbolism; in fact, they were actually three solid pieces of furniture with very specific positions in the layout of our Lodge.

It is interesting to note that this change gave the Wardens two columns each; but those standing on their pedestals are their personal emblems of office. Architecturally and Masonically speaking, the most important feature of King Solomon's Temple was without doubt the pair of pillars or columns at the porch. These twin pillars are now, as they have been for a very long time, familiar features in our Lodges, but their use is not uniform either in this country or elsewhere in the world.

A book, *Our Living Bible*, gives an authoritative account of Palestine archaeology. Completely independent of Masonic symbolism it describes the entrance to the Temple being flanked by two great bronze pillars, Jachin and

Boaz. The author has produced a drawing of the Temple, showing the pillars in detail. This is a visual record based on primitive paintings and reliefs found by archaeologists.

Reference to the two pillars is made in the I Kings 7:41, which I quote: "...the two Pillars, and the two bowls of the chapiters that were on the top of the two Pillars; and the two networks, to cover the two bowls of the chapiters which were upon the top of the Pillars."

The early Geneva Bible of 1560 illustrated a woodcut of the columns, surmounted by ornamental spheres. About this time, other illustrations were produced, showing the pillars surmounted by hemispheres or bowls. It is believed that the woodcut of the Geneva Bible was the result of mistaking two bowls, one superimposed on the other, for a globe.

It is interesting to note that the Hebrew word for the objects was goolah, meaning globes, bowls or vessels. There is, no doubt, an error in translation. We have only accepted the world as a sphere, and not as a flat surface, since about 1500; therefore it is fairly certain that the spheres on the original columns were certainly not maps, either celestial or terrestrial.

There has been speculation among Masonic, lay and clerical, writers alike as to whether the designation of the columns or pillars as 'right' and 'left' is from the viewpoint of the person entering or leaving the Temple. This question is generally pre-clouded in supposition which has frequently precluded any clear thinking on the subject. The pre-supposition in question is in connection with a subsidiary question of orientation that the Temple entrance faced east for which, it is true there are good, but not incontrovertible, arguments. In fact, the Bible is not certain on this subject. Likewise, many commentators have come to the conclusion that the columns in the porch were situated in the position shown here.

Such an arrangement is arrived at by equating the word 'right' with the geographical position 'South'; and 'left' with 'North'; for this there are good and sufficient reasons. It is well known that, in ancient times, the Hebrews referred to what we term the 'four cardinal points of the compass' from the position of a man looking towards the rising sun; so it is evident that the 'right hand' and the 'South' are synonymous terms. This view of the cardinal points is borne out by the *Encyclopedia Biblica* and again confirmed by Dr Kaufman in the *Jewish Encyclopedia*; both stating that 'East was called "the front"; the West, "the back"; the South the "right"; the North the "left"'.

The pillars, in the position as shown in the diagram above, must be assumed to be in the Biblical description; that is, the worshipper leaving the Temple and approaching the pillars from the inside. This attempted solution of the problem, in my opinion, is artificial. I consider one's first viewing of a building, or any of its external features, as the pillars must be assumed to be, to an observer

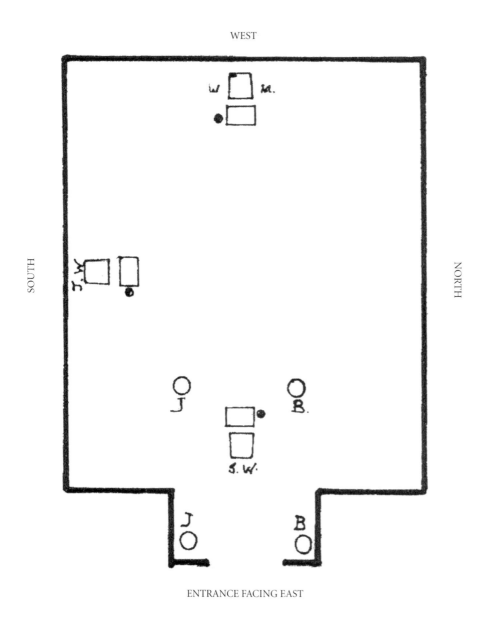

ENTRANCE FACING EAST

The Temple Facing East

approaching or viewing the building for the first time, must necessarily be from the outside. Otherwise, any discussion of these two pillars, from the standpoint of a worshipper leaving the Temple, is completely unrealistic; because, before he can leave the Temple, he must firstly have entered it!

The Temple may have faced west, which, in fact, the Bible has never explicitly denied. An interesting paragraph, to note from a novel called *Solomon and Sheba* in 1959 'And thus, at last, they came into the forecourt of the Temple, and up to the doors of the House of God. At the portals stood two columns, made by Huram-abi, cast in bronze six times the height of a man, from their bases to their great capitals, being decorated with lilies and two rows of pomegranates supporting a bowl; that on the right was called Jachin, that on the left was named Boaz.'

The first century AD historian Josephus clarifies the situation when he amplifies the Biblical description by saying that these pillars were set at the *entrance* of the porch etc. The addition of the one word 'entrance' would seem to put the matter beyond doubt; as one normally enters a Porch for the first time from the outside of a building; and here I refer to diagram A.

In early Operative Masonry, the Lodge was also the workshop, there being only one Warden in the Lodge his duty being to keep a smooth

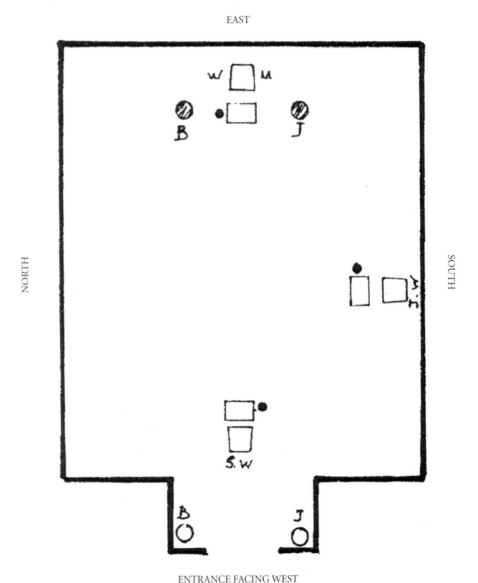

ENTRANCE FACING WEST

The Temple Facing West

progression of work and to act as a mediator in all disputes and to see that 'every Brother has had his due'. Refreshment was served in the Lodge room; the Warden used the column to indicate to the Brethren, amidst the noise of business, when to cease from labour and go to their refreshment. This he did by placing his column horizontally.

This practice continued up to the 1730s in Operative Masonry, at about which time Speculative Masonry Lodges appointed two Wardens. The Senior Warden, by ancient custom, was in charge of the Brethren while at work, and, in order to find a corresponding job for the Junior Warden, he was put in charge of the Brethren while at refreshment.

Between 1730 and 1760-1762 the Wardens were floor-officers, similar to today's Deacons. One thing is fairly certain – that the columns used were not their own personal emblems of office.

When the earliest surviving versions of the floor-cloths or tracingboards appeared, they included a drawing of an armillary sphere; this is a skeleton metal-ringed globe, the precursor of the celestial and terrestrial globes. These spheres, during the 18th and 19th centuries, were distinct features of English Lodge furniture; also illustrations of them are included (since 1819) in the Grand Lodge Certificate.

These globes depicted the terrestrial and celestial maps, intended to indicate the sun to rule the day and the moon to govern the night. Their use led to the evolution of the phrase 'Masonry Universal'; but the final change from these floor-spheres to the globes on the Wardens' columns cannot be dated precisely. It is possible that the globes with maps, on the Wardens' pedestal columns, were an economy measure to replace the expensive floor globes and ornamental stands. The term 'Masonry Universal' made its appearance in the Second Tracing Board in which the Masonic, and not the Biblical, description of Solomon's Pillars is given. After mentioning that they were made of molten brass, it states 'they were further adorned with spherical balls, on which were delineated maps of (a) the Celestial, and, (b) Terrestrial globes; pointing out Masonry Universal.

As the earth was believed to be flat at that time, the description of the globes surmounting the chapiters, as representing the two maps, is absolute nonsense; caused, no doubt, by some over-zealous Masonic script writer, trying to make the ritual comply with ill-founded theories. The explanation of the Second Tracing Board contains many other discrepancies, which, although not providing an entirely factual story, we now accept as traditional.

In 1760-1762, we have evidence of the Wardens, each carrying one of the pillars, namely Boaz and Jachin. The works *The Three Distinct Knocks* and *Jachin and Boaz* give the earliest descriptions of the raising and lowering of the Wardens' columns as follows:

1. The Senior and Junior Wardens each have a column approximately 20 inches long which are intended to represent the two columns at the porch of King Solomon's Temple, Boaz and Jachin.

2. Then the Junior Warden sets up his column whilst the Senior Warden lays his down; for the care of the Lodge is in the hands of the Junior Warden while they are at refreshment.

It is interesting to note that, before the Union of the two Grand Lodges in 1813, both Wardens sat in the West, where the Junior Deacon and the Inner Guard now sit. The raising and lowering procedure of the columns, the situation of the Wardens (as now known) were considered in 1810 by the Lodge of Promulgation, which, as no doubt you are aware, prepared the work on the Ritual for the Union of the two Grand Lodges; and they were subsequently authorised at the Union in 1813.

The present-day columns, which now stand on the Wardens' pedestals, were confirmed as emblems of the Wardens' offices, following a tradition of some two hundred years. An analysis of the history of the columns indicates:

1. That they should be identical, and represent the two bronze pillars at the porch of King Solomon's Temple.

CELESTIAL GLOBE
JUNIOR WARDEN'S COLUMN 'B'

TERRESTRIAL GLOBE
SENIOR WARDEN'S COLUMN 'J'

Celestial and Terrestrial Globes

2.   That the chapiters at the tops of the columns being so represented were of lilywork, network and pomegranates.

3.   That the two Wardens' columns do not represent Wisdom, Strength and Beauty or the Noble Orders, Doric and Corinthian.

4.   That the two original pillars were surmounted with bowls and not globes; although the globes as maps are now acceptable in the context of 'Masonry Universal'.

You are, no doubt, aware that the black night sky is on the celestial globe and that the celestial map, on the black background, depicts the stars in the universe. As regards the column on which the celestial map is fixed, to date no official ruling or explanation has been traced. One can look for an answer by inference.

1.   In the *Address on the Second Tracing Board* one reads that 'Those Pillars were further adorned with spherical balls, on which were delineated maps of the celestial (a) and terrestrial (b) globes, pointing out "Masonry Universal".' As the order of mention follows the names of the pillars, Boaz and Jachin in that order, one must assume that the celestial globe is on Boaz, or the Junior Warden's column.

2.   The standard *Address on the Presentation of the Grand Lodge Certificate* states that 'on the mosaic pavement are seen the Celestial and Terrestrial Globes'; this indicates again that the celestial map belongs to the Junior Warden's column.

3.   Again; on the certificate itself, a celestial floor globe is shown on the right hand side, together with furniture and jewels relating to the Junior Warden; that: is to say, the Corinthian column, plumb rule and the rough ashlar. The terrestrial globe is on the left, with the Doric column, level and smooth ashlar. Again, one must assume that the two pedestal columns do not form part of the three great columns of the Noble Orders which support our Lodge.

It should now be clear that the Wardens' columns wrongly represent the Doric and Corinthian Noble Orders of Architecture; as with the celestial globe being fixed to the Senior Warden's column, this, too, is incorrect, according to my foregoing research. I would suggest that the two maps should be reversed.

Expert opinion, from the editor of The Quatuor Coronati Lodge Correspondence Circle, which is associated with the Premier Lodge of Research, offers this advice:

1.   There is no official ruling about the style of the Wardens' columns.

2.   We are largely subject to the whims of the manufacturers regarding the styles.

3.   There is no justification for the Wardens' columns to represent the Doric, and Corinthian Noble Orders.

4.   To add globes to Doric and Corinthian Orders is definitely wrong.

5.   They should only be styled in accordance with the description given in the explanation of the Second Degree Tracing Board, which makes no reference to styles in Architecture.

6.   Whatever the design, Masonic records do not help to say which globe goes on which Column.

7.   Bro Walter Rodwell Wright (who was prominent in ritual matters at the time of the Union in 1813) said the columns were meant to represent the whole of creation, both celestial and terrestrial, but made no specific allocation to them.

8.   The Editor agrees that there is an argument for allocating the celestial globe to the Junior Warden, when considering the points put to him as outlined in this Lecture.

9.   As with many other matters, he said that the wishes of the majority of the Brethren in the Lodge should decide the allocation in the absence of any ruling from the Grand Master.

However, I would point out that the only drawing of the maps which I know of, and which has Grand Lodge approval, is the one on the Grand Lodge Certificate; and from their positions, in relation to the other items shown thereon, it is therefore reasonable to assume that Boaz and Junior Warden, with celestial, go together as do Jachin, Senior Warden and terrestrial.

Brethren, the assumptions and opinions I have expressed in the Lecture are a result of my own researches and are not offered as official answers. Architectural language has no exact counterpart, for the very good reason that, while its roots are in the ancient world, many of its latest expressions are still precisely those which that world evolved and crystalised.

Classical architecture needs to be understood in a large and general way, as the most comprehensive and stable manner of design the world has ever seen. Therefore we cannot exclude the classical past from our experience in architecture, any more than we can in literature or art; it is a part of us in Freemasonry. If the forms in which it is presented tend now to have something of the obscurity of a 'dead' language, then, Brethren, I suggest you should learn the language.

CHAPTER 3

Some Symbols of the First Degree

Symbols are outward signs of an inward and spiritual concept representing to us the world of reality and forming a link with the unseen world, presenting truth in a concrete form, awakening in us a more developed state of consciousness, made by creative thought: ritual symbolism.

Thomas Carlyle said in *Sartor Resartus*, that:

'*By symbols is man guided and commanded, made happy, made wretched. He everywhere finds himself encompassed with symbols recognised as such or not recognised; the Universe is but one vast symbol of God, nay. If thou will have it, what is man but a symbol of God; is not all that he does symbolical; a revelation of sense of the Mystic God-given force that is in him, a Gospel of Freedom, which he, the Messiah of nature, preaches, as he can by word and act. Not a hut he builds but is the visible embodiment of a thought, but bears record of invisible things, but is, in the transcendental sense, symbolic as well as real. What a man believes, lays to heart, and acts upon, concerning this mysterious universe and his duty and destiny in it, that, determines all the rest and is his religion.*'

Our candidate is about to forge a link with the 'infinite' and join in the Ideals of the Brotherhood of human dignity and freedom with one limit to liberty that is, the liberty of the other man and the happiness of all.

To begin at the beginning. A nervous, apprehensive figure of a man stands dishevelled, ill-shod and blind before a door; a door which is fast shut and firmly locked against him. His companion, standing beside him, takes him by the right wrist, and, guiding his right hand to the knocker, tells him to strike the door before him, slowly and deliberately, three times. The Ceremony of his Initiation has begun.

The word 'initiation' comes from the Latin, and means 'a beginning'. The word 'candidate' also comes from Latin and originally meant 'clothed in blinding white' from the custom of Roman candidates for public office being obliged to wear a white robe, the 'toga Candida'. The Masonic candidate is a man who requests the favour of a Degree, or one who aspires to one. Some of the older writings, particularly in France, speak of the uninitiated as 'profane' that is, a heathen, a man not initiated into religious rites; or one who is outside the Temple.

A candidate for Freemasonry must be of good reputation and integrity, and well fitted to become a member of the Lodge in which he seeks Initiation. He must be a free man, of twenty-one years, and the tongue of good report must have been heard in his favour. He must be well and worthily recommended, and must have been regularly proposed and approved in open Lodge. He must come of his free-will and accord, humbly soliciting to be admitted to the mysteries and privileges of Freemasonry. He will be asked to make a solemn affirmation that he puts his trust in God; and he must, at the right time and in the right way, be presented to the Lodge; to show that is a fit and proper person to be made a Freemason.

'He must be a free man and of the age of twenty-one years.' A bondman was tied to his Master and a son to his father; if he were less than twenty-one years old he might be repossessed and made to reveal the secrets of Masonry. At twenty-one a man was legally an adult; a minimum age that anyone might be Initiated into the Craft. Undergraduates at the University Lodges of Oxford and Cambridge Apollo and Isaac Newton have no right to be initiated at eighteen, but in every case a dispensation must be applied for.

'He must come of his own free-will and accord uninfluenced by mercenary or any other unworthy motive.' No pressure from friends, or employers, must be used; and it must be entirely voluntary without a thought of financial reward, showing that the aspirant has reached the right stage of mental advancement.

'He must be of honest parentage.' We must assume that young men of illegitimate birth were not acceptable to the Guilds or trade fraternities of the Middle Ages, whether Masonic or otherwise. This may have been the result of priestly influences of early Jewish and Christian refusal to admit bastards into the priesthood, based on the ruthless verse in the *Book of Deuteronomy,* 'A bastard shall not enter into the Congregation of the Lord; even to his tenth generation.' The 'Steinmetzen', the German Stonemasons required that the prospective Apprentice prove that he was of legitimate birth.

The Operative Freemasons would take no one who had a bodily blemish. This had many obvious practical considerations, for he would be called upon to do work demanding strength and agility, moving heavy blocks of stone with the use of simple tackle. Any youth, physically unequal to such tasks, might soon have found himself broken, and thereby put his Brethren at risk, as well as being a burden on his Lodge, or on his Lord who employed him. During the 19th century, the Craft looked on the matter more humanely so long as the blemish did not render him incapable of learning the Art, any man might become a Mason. The Grand Secretary, in a letter dated 15th March 1902, said that the fact that a candidate had no thumb would not bar his admittance, provided that he was a satisfactory candidate in every other way.

The Ceremony is a series of Three of Trinities, Three Ks., Steps, Lights, Greater and Lesser, Columns, Parts of Time, Tools, Secrets, Staves, Rungs, Principal Officers, Assistant Officers, Dangers, three sides of the strongest structural form – a Triangle of Force in each case. The candidate comes to our Lodge and outside the door he meets the Tyler, the Mason who by his presence covers the sacred precincts from all intrusion. There he is prepared in the classical sense the word 'candidate' means 'one clothed in a white garment'. With his preparation completed, the ceremony itself can begin and by the candidate himself with Three Distinct Knocks upon the door of the Lodge spaced well apart from each other.

So what do these knocks signify? The triple knock refers to three doors; one real, two symbolic. As the Evangelist Saint John says; 'Behold, I stand at the door and knock. If any man hears my voice and opens the door, I will come in to him, and I will sup with him, and he with me.' In Operative Lodges the triple knock was the symbol of the Triune; GodFather, Son and Holy Ghost. The Lectures and old Catechisms tell us that they allude to an ancient and venerable exhortation, mentioned in the Gospels of both Matthew and Luke: 'Seek, and ye shall find; Ask, and ye shall receive; Knock, and it shall be opened unto you.' They also allude to the virtues of Faith, Hope and Charity; not only of gifts of money, but a Brother should be prepared to give time and effort to his Brethren when they have need of it. As the Ritual says: 'and part in serving a friend of Brother in time of need, without detriment to myself or connections'.

The Door of the Lodge is of great importance; it has of course, two sides so it faces both ways; its outer face looks on the profane world and its other face looks into the Lodge where we conduct all our private business, hopefully after leaving our worldly cares on the other side of the door. The Roman god Janus, after whom the month of January is named, was also a god of change; much like the Hindu god Shiva. Statues of Janus show him with one head and two faces; he looks back on the Old Year and, at the same time, looks forward to the new. Not only were doors sacred to him, but the hinges which secured it to its frame. Going through a spiritual door hopefully represents a change for the better; and it should be with this very much in mind that the door of the Lodge will open for the candidate, and initiate the process of spiritual change and growth. It must therefore be with faith in the Lord God, for a new beginning, and with hope and charity in his heart that a candidate knocks to gain admission on the first of three doors, through which he will pass. The password which gains him entry is the 'Tongue of Good Report'.

So much for his *mental* preparation; now let's look at his *physical*.

It is appropriate that Initiates in many Lodges wear a suit of white pyjamas, white being an emblem of innocence, and white because he is indeed a candidate for Initiation. Normally candidates have their trouser legs and shirt sleeves rolled up, which wrecks pressed shirts and trousers! Seriously though, putting a candidate into a suit of pyjamas can solve several problems. Leaving aside the removal of signet and wedding rings, the purists of the 18th century were concerned with metal buttons and buckles. While these are most unlikely to be given 'in the cause of Masonic Charity', in the ancient world all metal belonged to the gods of the Underworld; they should never be brought into the Lodge by an Initiate. Sleeves and legs of pyjamas can be permanently adjusted so that safety pins don't have to be used; metal again.

The candidate is hoodwinked so that in the unlikely event of his escaping from the Lodge before the ceremony has been completed, he would be unable to tell anyone about its interior. It also symbolises his progress from 'darkness to light'; as we read in the lectures, 'that my heart might conceive before my eyes should discover'. It is also emblematic, perhaps, of the trust that every candidate should have in his proposer and seconder, and in friends and relatives in the Craft. All of us, from the Grand Master to the newest Entered Apprentice, have made the same journey which he is about to undertake.

His right arm is made bare to show that he is fit for manual labour, and that he carries no concealed weapons. He was defenceless; he had no need of arms as he came in peace of his own free-will and accord. This had meaning two hundred years ago but less so these days; it would be stupid and pointless for an Operative Lodge to employ a cripple 'perfect in his parts and honourable to the builder' for he would be unfit for work, a danger to his brethren on the building site and a liability on the Lodge's charity box.

His left breast is made bare principally to uncover the heart, and to show the Brethren that he is not a woman. It would be interesting to see if any women take this, as a test case, to the High Court and claim sexual discrimination. How, I wonder, would Grand Lodge counter this argument? Much more likely is the universal tradition that the heart is the seat of the soul and it suggests the candidate's fervency, zeal and insincerity. But perhaps a better test of his sex might be to introduce him naked; but I have not been able to find any instance of this practice in the ancient world, even though all Greek males exercised in the nude. His heart is also effectually exposed, to show that it is 'in the right place', and it is open to receive instruction from his elders and betters in the Craft; and it will shortly be tried with points of both the poignard and the compasses, symbolising the prick of conscience.

His left knee is bare so that when he takes his Great and Solemn Obligation his body will be in contact with Mother Earth; or it would be if it were not for the kneeling stool. 'For dust thou art and to dust shalt thou return' as the Christian burial service puts it.

His right heel is slipshod as evidence of the candidate's humility. It came to Masonry from folklore, especially Jewish tradition where it was a gesture of reverence. Moses was instructed to 'put off thy shoes from thy feet for the place thou standest is holy ground'. The Greek hero Jason—who led the Argonauts in the Quest for the Golden Fleece—came before Pelias the Usurper without a sandal on his left foot. He had been warned in a dream that a man thus shod would appear and overthrow him. Such details were pregnant without meaning. He is, effectively, off-balance and would find running away difficult; notice how balance is achieved in subsequent degrees; 'neither turning to the right nor to the left from the strict path of virtue.' This was a testimony in Israel (*Deuteronomy, chapter 23:5-10*).

This is called the 'Rite of Discalceation' that is giving testimony of sincerity of intention. In Scotland in the First Degree the VSL is open at *Ruth 4:7-8*, and when the candidate is standing in the NE Corner, he is asked to take off his shoe and hand it to the WM; verses 7 and 8 are then read to him, and the Brethren are called to witness that he has entered Freemasonry and is ratifying the bargain with the Lodge; his shoe is then returned to him.

He is hoodwinked. Candidates in all the Mysteries were required to be blindfolded. It is also an emblem not only of secrecy but of the darkness which vanishes in the Light of Initiation. The poet Milton wrote 'What in me is dark, illumine; what is low, raise and support.' This is the prayer of every candidate. The Greek Philosopher Plato said that, 'the ignorant suffer from ignorance, as the blind man for want of sight'.

A cable tow with a running noose was placed about his neck. It serves to remind him of the mortality of life; and the wearing of a halter by an Initiate harks back to the Mysteries, now lost in antiquity. In the Zoroastrian system, some three thousand years ago, everyone was thought to have a noose about his neck, which at death fell from a righteous man, but dragged the wicked man down to hell.

It is of interest to hear that in the Dutch Lodge in South Africa a candidate enters a Chamber of Preparation, signs his declaration and is left for a considerable time, to rest his mind.

Then he is led to another Chamber of Meditation where he sits in a chair and before him is a dimly lighted transparency, 'Man know Thyself'.

Then in a Third Chamber, or Silence, he acknowledges the Fatherhood of God and the Brotherhood of Man, and is taught that silence is symbolical of the great secrecy which every Freemason must observe as regards what he sees and hears within the Temple.

His attention is drawn to the figure of an owl, emblematic of watchfulness. He is handed bread dipped in salt to eat and water to drink. He then enters the Lodge for the ceremony.

The Ks are given and he stands ready to enter the unknown; the vibrations are answered, the barrier is removed and he stands before the Lodge. In an old phraseology three Ks or the candidate (the Tyler should hold the candidate's hand in such a position that it is he, the candidate, who knocks for himself) were said to be the three Masonic messages to all humanity.

Seek, and ye shall find. Ask, and ye shall have. Knock, and it shall be opened unto you.

When the candidate is admitted by the Inner Guard, he's tried by the point of a sharp instrument which is presented to his naked left breast. The stiletto or poignard is a narrow dagger, with a cross-hilt, twice illustrated in the Collar Jewel of the Inner Guard. If it is held downwards by the blade, it forms the Christian emblem of the cross, as a Tyler should carry his sword inside the Lodge. It symbolises Peace. Our Operative forebears used the 'brickie's trowel', still a sharp instrument. It used to be the Collar Jewel of the youngest Apprentice, 'who kept the door'. It serves the same purpose and it is razor sharp. The trowel today has been largely ignored by the Speculative Freemason. Its position has been reduced to that of the Collar Jewel of the Charity Steward; a heart might be better? The candidate is reminded that he is about to embark on something sacred and solemn. It emphasises the difficulty of entrance, in more than one sense.

In medieval times, the possibility of an evil spirit impersonating a human being was very firmly held by all sorts of people and the infallible means of frightening him away was to confront him with the sign of the cross. As mentioned previously, if the poignard is held upright by the blade, it forms a cross. At the height of the idea of medieval Chivalry, a squire spent the night before his investiture on his knees in prayer, before the high altar in the chapel, holding his sword in this manner.

The candidate is then instructed to kneel and receive the benefit of Masonic prayer; or to 'stand covered' if Jew, Muslim or Parsee. The Deacons cross their wands over his head, forming an upright triangle, emblematic of fire. Perhaps this indirectly refers to the Christian 'Feast of Pentecost', where tongues of fire representing the Holy Spirit descended from heaven on all those present. The Bishop's mitre represents these 'tongues of flame'. The Deacons also cross their wands over the candidate's head when he takes his Obligation; again the upright fire triangle.

He kneels in prayer and affirms his trust in God. One old Lancashire Working says, 'Mr. ******. It is only fair to inform you that one, holding a drawn sword, is before you; and one, holding the cable tow about your neck is behind you. In this position, of difficulty and danger, in whom do you put your trust?' So the candidate is in very real and actual danger here.

The 'Sign of Prayer' is a most ancient gesture, and is given by placing your hand upon the heart with the four fingers, and the thumb, held parallel. Any other Sign and we've all seen it, haven't we, is incorrect. The Sign is discharged by dropping it; it should never be cut, as it is not a Masonic sign. Then he is instructed to rise.

He now commences on the 'Rite of Circumambulation', part of a very old ceremony carrying on the mystic sodalities of the ancient civilisations in the course of the sun; if you would do reverence you must turn towards your right hand. In the old days the Rite of Circumambulation was rather different to ours, a clear space is left around the outside of the Lodge this space being the outer path and he was conducted to each gate and after reception he was allowed on to the inner floor of the Lodge and passed round the inner path to show that he is properly prepare. Thus was emphasised the gates of entry, guarded by the S and JWs and that only when he has passed these points was he admitted to the presence of the WM. He will trace this course again throughout his Masonic career following the Ritual of the neophytes of the Druids at Stonehenge or the Prophets of Baal on Mount Carmel.

In primitive times this was known as the Rite of the Mystic Journey and described thus: 'The Candidate begins to approach the East by way of the North, the place of Darkness and Fear on to the opposite the South, the place of the sun, of High Twelve the scene of the labours, thence to the West, being the place of Closing standing for Rest the place for finishing and for presentations. The East being the Glorious Centre with the Star lighting the South, the Great Dawn of Joy'. In some of these old initiations they speak of 27 circumambulations, each round of which contained on its path a 'test' for the initiate.

The JD takes him round the Lodge and he Ks. at the W's gate and he is found 'Free and of Good Report' and receives the grip of Fellowship which should be strong and reassuring; it is the first actual physical contact with the Lodge via the JW and then the SW presents him to the WM.

He takes his Solemn Declarations.

The JD Instructs him in the Ad.. .the Ss of Evolution, each of which carry him forward further than the previous one, something has been gained and nothing has been lost: symbolically his will to go has increased as his trust is so well placed.

In the old rituals the Ss. are said to be 9, 12 and 15 inches—so a yard away from the kneeling stool Bro JD.

His right hand is on the VSL while his left is employed in supporting in the form of a Sq. (which is his correct position of the points) that the love of virtue may be centred in his heart.

He is obligated beneath the crossed wands of the S and JDs, representing thereby the triangular door of the ancient Egyptian Lodge and the second of the symbolical portals through which he has to pass (the first was at the prayer and the third is the portal through which he will pass out as a Bro) and he sees *light* which is restored to him, his eyes being fixed on the VSL, the greatest and truest guide for our Fraternity, with the square and compasses, symbols of revelation and creation.

Some Lodges have the VSL open at Psalm 133, but if it be open at any of its pages it is perfectly in order. The VSL was in use in 1600 from an old

Obligation; 'So help me G. and the Holy contents of this BOOK.'

Brethren, to Freemasons the VSL be it the Bible of the Christian, the Qur 'an of the Muslim, the *Zend Avesta* of the Parsee, the *Veda* of the Hindu, or the *Tripitaka* of the Buddhist is the symbol of the Word of God, the Universal Father of all Mankind, who speaks to His children through many prophets in many tongues.

It may be of interest to quote the experiences of a Bro who visited a Lodge in Bombay—he related that, when he attended an Initiation Ceremony, there were five bibles on the altar the M. was a Muslim, one of the candidates who received the First Degree was a Parsee and the other a Hindu. The work was done in English in a dignified and impressive manner (the author's Lodge has three bibles).

After sealing his Great and Solemn Obligation on the VSL he is restored to light, the hoodwink is dramatically removed in a clap of thunder; the Master and Wardens making the triangle, an upright one, in the air, with their gavels, before the Great Knock. Other versions represent the lightning flash; zigzag motion, a sudden lightning-strike and its roll of thunder. The whole represents inspiration; literally 'an indrawn breath'; the triangle is another representation of the Trinity but an upright triangle is also a representation of fire, the burning and consuming element; the fire that purges and purifies the Soul, as metal is refined in a furnace. Note that it is the Deacon, man's higher self, who actually removes the hoodwink and physical light is restored to the candidate's eyes; at last he can see the now-familiar Three Great Emblematic Lights of Freemasonry, the VSL, the Square and the Compasses. Their symbolism is now explained. The VSL contains everything for Man's salvation. The square and the compasses are to be his guide on Earth. The angle of the square is fixed and immutable but the compasses will adjust to any angle. I suggest that the correct way round for the VSL to be is so that the candidate can see and read it, the angle of the square pointing towards him. This is the exact opposite of Emulation Working. The reason I suggest this way is so that the candidate can *actually* see that it is not just any nicely bound book.

It is then that the WM says 'Rise D. ob Bro. a g MS'. This is the moment that he is a Bro. He is raised to his feet by the Master and his shoe is returned with an explanation; he discovers the Three Lesser Lights, the Master and his Wardens. He is told that the Senior Warden represents the sun, the spirit of man; and the Junior Warden represents the moon, the intuitive soul of man. The dangers are now explained and again there are three. The cross of the poignard is shown again; the cable tow of ignorance is removed, and cast aside. He is born again and he has no need of an umbilical cord.

Of the secrets much could be said; suffice it to say that much has been written but unless you have come by them in a legal manner, the whole mystique is missing: I might read the text in English, as I don't read Hebrew of the Bar Mitzvah, but that does not make me a Son of the Covenant. Jewish Brethren may read the Confirmation Service in the *Book of Common Prayer*, but that does not mean they may make their communion at the altar rail.

The entire world knows that we have a *sign*, a *grip* or *token*, and a *word*. The meaning of the sign is straightforward: it displays the severing of man's divine and earthly parts. What isn't generally realised is that the Due Guard beloved of our Scottish and American Brethren has disappeared. The hand is thrust forward, in Emulation Working, though it is never explained; but this must be a pale shadow of the Due Guard, which appears in the Royal Arch, again unexplained.

The wording of the penalty in the First Degree runs something like this: 'being branded a wilfully perjured individual, devoid of all moral worth; and totally unfit to be received into this worshipful Lodge, or any other warranted Lodge or society of men, who prize honour and virtue above the external advantages of rank and fortune'. Very nice; but consider; branding was a mark of slavery and of theft in the ancient and medieval world; usually implanted on forehead or cheek. It is surely not the mark of a 'free man'?

There are three phrases to be examined in this Obligation.

a) ytca.

This alludes to the Penal Sign of the Degree. It severs the Upper Nature of Man from the Lower, or baser. Hopefully we cultivate the former, and suppress, or better still, destroy the latter. Never mind the rest of the Penalty; if carried out literally, there is no need of anything else! This represents the severing of the Divine and human parts of man, the head from the body, Man's better nature from his baser.

b) yttobtr.

This won't actually kill you, but you won't be able to make an intelligent sound for the rest of your natural life. You will certainly be unable to plead your cause before the Throne of Heavenly Grace.

c) bbitsots, alwm, oaclfts, wttreaftitfh.

Let us examine the state of the ground. It is neither Sea, nor is it Dry Ground. It will certainly never be consecrated. Only in recent memory have suicides been permitted to be buried in Consecrated Ground; and a Burial Service could only be conducted with the corpse actually present. I get the distinct impression that the remains of a wilfully perjured Freemason would be shovelled into a hole in the ground in the middle of the night.

In the old Operative working the G. was to be 'concealed', the S. to be 'heled' and the word never to be 'revealed'.

In the *Cooke MS.* of 1490 the word 'hele' appears and is interpreted as 'must conceal'.

The wisdom of the old times records: 'Offer not your right hand easily to everyone, do not draw up nor endeavour to raise by extending your right hand to the unadopted and uninitiated.'

Among the Ancient peoples the Hand was the symbol of the Builders and in their very early art the Supreme Being was frequently depicted by a Hand extending from a Cloud In the act benediction. The right hand is said to be the emblem of *fidelity*, the left, symbolical of *equity*. The grip or token is a means of recognition, together with the sign and word. The word, as we all know, is B. But before the Union in 1813 the Ancients accused the Moderns of interchanging the Secrets of the two Degrees which they had done in response to a series of articles, published in *The Morning Post* in October 1730. The story we find in the VSL at *II Kings 10:3* describes how one day King Jehu was driving his chariot along an eastern road and on approaching Jehonadab, Son of Rechab, who was walking towards him, he stepped down and greeted him thus: 'Is thy heart right, as my heart is with thy heart?" Jehonadab answered "It is." Then said the King: "If it be, give me thine hand," and he gave him his hand and he took up into the chariot. That, I believe, is the first instance on record of a hand-grip used to cement a bond or brotherhood and friendship and the sign of mutual heart sympathy.

The s the g the w...s, by which we greet each other, should not be the whole of Masonry, but the overflowing passion for that for which Masonry exists: the building of man. The formal acts they represent may still be important to us, as revelations of the Ancient Law, but there is something which they represent that is far greater, something they do not express, that far transcends in importance word and sign perfection the use of heart and hand; in the gathering of the great stones, the powers of society and mankind, of which we build again the Temple that has crumbled by the neglect of man, and yet more the Temple that is in the heavens higher still, than the wildest concept of those who have toiled, day and night, in all ages of Masonry, in order to ensure the accurate submission of man to the Divine Law, to try to live, and by that life to fill the world with an atmosphere which is a conscience, an influence not seen but felt, that does not rival, but fills all, pervades all, and leads to eternal Brotherhood.

But *knowing* the correct word is one thing; how to use it quite another. In the days of the Operatives, a strange Brother, looking for work on the site of a cathedral, would have been proved. The actual sign, token and word were proof of his professional skills as they were entrusted after much labour; and proof of actual skills being difficult to cart about! A Mason will be proved in the same way today, an added requirement being the Grand Lodge Certificate, and sometimes some proof of payment of Lodge dues especially in the United States may be required.

The candidate is taught how to prove himself as an Entered Apprentice and is properly called upon by the Wardens. He is then invested with the pure white apron the skin of a lamb the emblem of purity and innocence, the Lamb of God. Pure white, the lambskin apron will take any mark, for good or ill. In America, this white lambskin apron is never worn again; it is carried at the Brother's funeral, and buried with him. When I visited The Evangelist Lodge No 600 in New York in 1976, I thought how well off they were for Entered Apprentices. It turned out that they were Past Masters, wearing another white apron, not their own. They looked at my regalia with some interest, but found it strange that I had no Initiate's apron of my own.

The Initiate is now placed in the North-East part of the Lodge and here the authors' Lodge uses a symbol from Bristol Working. The Rough Ashlar is placed between his feet, which are squared round the stone. The Lectures tell us, 'The Rough Ashlar is a stone, rough and unhewn as taken from the quarry; until by the industry and ingenuity of the workman it is modelled, wrought into due form and rendered fit for the intended structure. This represents to us the mind of man, in his infant or primitive state, rough and unpolished as that stone; until by the kind care of his parents or guardians in giving him a liberal and virtuous education, his mind is cultivated and he comes a fit member of civilised society.' The North-East is traditionally the beginning of any Work, and is the first part of the building's foundations illumined by the rays of the rising sun.

He receives the Charity Charge here to show his duty to his Brethren and his obligation to relieve the poor and distressed. But faith and hope are not mentioned here as they are in the First Degree Tracing Board and in the Rose Croix and charity is purely financial; not the Greek word *agape*, love for all mankind. 'Faith, Hope and Charity; these three [note three again] and the greatest of these is Charity' said the blessed Apostle Saint Paul. 'And cheerfully embrace the opportunity of *practising* that virtue, which you now profess to admire,' as the ritual puts it.

The candidate is then presented with the Working Tools. In reality, the Operative Apprentice would have been instructed in the uses of more tools than these – axes, hammers, mauls; chisels, callipers and gauges, squares and bevels, rasps, scrapers; and so on. The Mason who builds a wall whatever his grade must have had lines, levels, plumbs, trowels, hammers and so on, to enable him to build true and square, on the foundations set out with enormous care by the foreman or Master Builder. In the Bristol Working when the candidate returns to the Lodge, having restored his personal comforts, he is told to sit at a table and to write the word. If he attempts to do so, a gong is sounded and discord from the organ makes a din his fingers are rapped and he is shown a man with his T. cut across. His proper answer should be 'I was told to be c.'

On his return his attention is directed to 'The Ancient Charge; founded on the Excellencies of the Institution, and the Qualification of its members. Emulation calls it 'Charge after Initiation,' without even an article in front of it. Its origin goes back at least to the 12th Century and at the end he is enjoined to endeavour to make a daily advancement in Masonic knowledge'.

Our Ancient Charge depicting the duties of the Bros, of the Mystic Tie the Threefold Tie uniting man with God, his fellowmen and with himself linking his life with the eternal enterprise breaking the loneliness and organising us in spiritual faith and a common high endeavour whose golden rule is: 'Help me to need no aid from men, that I may aid such men as need.'

Our ceremonies are parts of an orderly tradition, unfolding through the centuries and emanating from the ancient secret Fraternities perpetuating the esoteric doctrines of antiquity for I believe civilisation is unfolding to a predetermined plan, part of which – and an essential part – is the discipline of each of us so that we can contribute to the final perfection of the whole by our influence in act and deed by that spiritual communion of our great Brotherhood.

Thus we extend our congratulations and always receive with acclamation every newly made Bro and we trust that the tessellated pavement will ever remain to him as bright as when it first came from the quarries of truth the jewels ever brighten at his touch and the Great Lights remain undimmed and undecayed to eternity.

To every candidate I would say, 'Keep on asking the question why?' To every experienced Craftsman, I would say the same. But, my experienced Brethren, you have the advantage of being Master Masons and you can go to various textbooks and rituals, as well as to your own version of the VSL, and seek the answers you are looking for. But the poor Entered Apprentice has virtually nothing to help him for he is allowed no ritual book and is often fobbed off with half-answers. If you don't know the answer, have the courage to say so; even better, find out! Give him an answer which will stand up in the light of later knowledge. Grand Lodge has an excellent library and people are there to help you answer anything you care to ask them.

What does the average Lodge do with its Past Masters when they have left office as IPM? Might I suggest that they look after one of the younger, less experienced Brethren? They should answer his questions on our ritual and history and teach him Mason jurisprudence. I was fortunate in having such a teacher and it stood me in good stead when I became Master for the first time. The Irish and Scots call them 'intendents'; they do the pupil's work on the night should he be unable to come to the Meeting at the last moment and it's useful for the Director of Ceremonies as he does not have to find an 'extra' to fill gaps. I can promise any intendent an 'interesting time'.

CHAPTER 4

Masonic Remains Found
at Pompeii, 1874

In the year 1874 certain excavations at Pompeii were carried out by the Italian Government under the direction of Signor Fiorelli, which led to the locality of the Porta Stabiana, the most ancient, be it said, of all the gates in the walls of the town, and close to the quarters of the leather manufacturers (*officina coriariorum*). Here were discovered the stone slabs of a roof, and then the capitals of certain columns bearing traces of fire, and other indications clearly pointing to the fact that a temple or hall of some sort had been destroyed here in the great eruption of the year AD79. After some further work the excavators removed a large heap of lava ashes, cinders and detritus no less than 19ft in depth, with the result that there came to light the remains of a building which evidently had been erected for some special cult.

On referring to the outline plan, some idea of its formation can be obtained. The area laid bare was about 60ft square, whilst seven columns, some 15ft in height, occupied the position indicated, forming, it will be observed, two sides of a square.

In advance of the last of the seven columns to the left, two more were discovered, facing a stone pedestal 4ft high. The ashes and cinders etc. which had been lying on it were removed, and then, after a period of 1,795 years' seclusion from the eye of man, there stood revealed a specimen of mosaic art which, from its remarkable formation and wonderful symbolism, may be considered justly as unique, not only in /masonry, but also in Archaeology.

It formed the top of a pedestal, being in size slightly over a foot square, and fixed now in a stout frame of wood it is to be seen in the National Museum at Naples. The background, bearing traces of exposure to tremendous heat, is of a grey greenish stone, in the centre of which is depicted a human skull, remarkably correct in its material details, the teeth, nostrils, eye sockets, etc. being rendered with fidelity and distinctness.

Above the skull is what at first sight purports to be a square rule of brown wood with brass tips, but it is interesting to note that the angle formed is not 90 degrees, as if to suggest that the trained hand of a Master Mason is required to adjust it. Below is figured a level, similarly tinted to represent wood and brass. The position of the square and level makes a triangle from the apex of which a plum-line depends, whence is suspended the skull, below which we find a wheel, furnished with six spokes, which, however, clearly by design, do not meet at the centre. On the upper rim is represented a butterfly, one of the

Tracing Board Found at Pompeii, 1874

Egyptian emblems of resurrection, having wings of a reddish-brown colour, edged with yellow and dotted with blue.

Particularly noticeable is the symmetry of the design, for if the plumb line be extended, the skull, wings and wheel are divided into two equal parts, showing that the scheme is just true and perfect according to Masonic rule.

Passing to the symbols on each side we find a very remarkable and delicately balanced antithesis.

On the right is a gnarled staff, which I suggest may be that of a pilgrim, from which a coarse, rough piece of cloth, in yellow, grey and brown colours, is depicted, fastened by a ribbon. Above it appears a leathern wallet which, like the rough staff, may well be deemed part of a pilgrim's homely equipment.

On the left we find what evidently is a spear, or sceptre, standing upright, and having the butt or tip of iron.

From the middle of this spear there hang, fastened by a cord of gold, what seem to be robes of scarlet and purple.

Towards the crown, or point, the sceptre is covered with white cord-braid of a diamond pattern.

The fuller significance, however, of this sceptre and the royal robes appears hardly suitable for a written description, though it is obvious to all companions of the R.A.

From the position of the shadow depicted on the mosaic it will be seen that the sun is shining upon the higher and royal emblems, whilst the symbols of death, resurrection and eternity separate the tokens of this world's pilgrimage from those of another and brighter state.

A matter of surpassing interest was the discovery of a convenient room adjoining the lodge, as shown on the plan to the left of the pedestal, which curiously enough revealed traces of frescos in the true Masonic blue; and if, as it seemed, there was no access of light, the candidate or neophyte in this room must have been kept in a state of darkness before admission to the light and knowledge

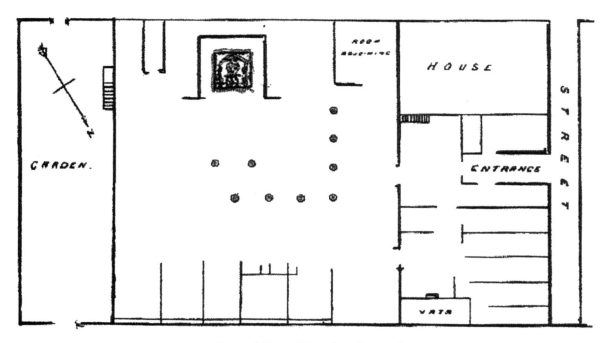

Ground Plan of Temple at Pompeii

of the lodge. On the walls of this smaller room were discovered several *graffiti*, or wall writings, consisting chiefly of triangles, squares and compasses.

From the position of the room, and its proximity to the actual lodge, there is no doubt that if, as I surmise, the candidate was placed within it at the commencement of the ceremony of initiation, he, on leaving it, at once must have been confronted with the emblem of mortality that is displayed on the mosaic I have described.

Having proceeded thus far, the question of origin very naturally arises, and as to this it appears without doubt that the pedestal table and lodge are those of one of the Hetaeriae, or secret societies, with which Pompeii was honeycombed to a greater extent than even Rome. Flourishing everywhere, even the Caesars dreaded their power.

To such an extent had their influence spread, especially in elections, that on one occasion at least, a special commission was sent from Rome to examine into the matter, without, however, any definite result, and more than one decree of the Roman Senate, in Collegiis illicitis, was issued against the Hetaeriae, only to prove as abortive as centuries later those Papal thunderbolts of Christian Rome which were hurled against modern Freemasonry.

In conclusion, may I add that whilst I do not seek to prove a Masonic Lodge, such as we know it, was flourishing at Pompeii in the year AD74 , on the other hand the singularly symbolic nature of the pedestal-top, whereon so many of the principal emblems of our craft are depicted conspicuously, the features of the lodge itself, and the place where it was discovered, are sufficient to create the liveliest interest in the least imaginative of Masonic minds, for there is no doubt of their significance, and they have been kept beneath tons of lava and ashes for nearly 1,800 years, under circumstances forming an absolute guarantee of their genuineness.

Surely if there lingers yet any doubt as to the antiquity of Freemasonry, it must be dispelled to some extent by these Pompeian relics of our Craft.

Chapter 5

Symbolism of the Second Degree

Masonry, more than any other system of philosophy, morality or religion, brings home to the individual the importance of symbolism, therefore it is time well spent for any mason to study not only the symbolism of masonry but also the symbolism of life.

The young Pharaoh with his left foot forward appears on the dais and is being presented by someone probably Isis as the Universal Mother with the Master's Grip, the symbol of life. The Crux Ansata appears in the other hand. Above are the Cartouches with the names of the ruler.

The Director of Ceremonies leads the salutation of the Brethren. These appear in two layers, the Above and the Below (Pairs of Opposites). The good and the evil are symbolised by the masks of Harmachis for Osiris-Horus (the Hawk) and Anubis for Set (the Jackal); all with a Sign, well known to the Craft.

The First Degree representing the entry of all men into mortal existence by preparation and discipline the special objective of the Second Degree becomes possible namely contemplation and enlightenment; the striving by work and development of a Brother's faculties until he realises that he will connect with, and ultimately terminate in, the Divine.

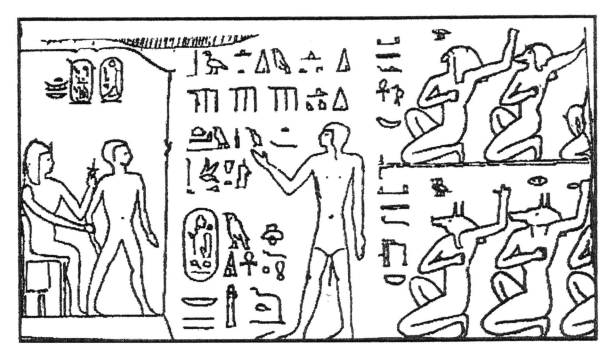

Illustration of a Stone in Bath Museum 133BC

The Second Degree is by no means as uninteresting as a superficial examination of it has often led Brethren to suppose. It symbolises a long course of personal developmental, requiring deep study and an ever-growing knowledge of the mental and physical sides of his natures.

Having received 'Light' around him, he is now to illumine the darkness within. It is for this purpose he was taught how to calm his mind, to free it from all vain and unbecoming thoughts to knock off superfluous knobs and excrescences to concentrate and to contemplate. In one of the old schools of thought it is called the 'Focus Degree'.

In olden times, three Temples were used, one for each ceremony. Over the door of the Second Temple were five stars; inside the square, the level and the plumb rule.

Passing means a midway or transitional phase of Life the first phase in the olden times being 'Darkness of Natural Reason' and the second, 'Illumination of the Mind', and the third, 'Light of the Spirit'.

You have heard how it is that we emphasise the distribution of spiritual force and how we secure the idea of ascending to higher levels by progressively opening up from one Degree to another and exposing in each a Tracing Board. So in this Degree it is the IPM who finally seals the opening by placing the square and compasses.

The WM still represents the 'Rising Sun', coming from the East. In the Indian ritual he is Brahma, the Creator and rising sun. In Egyptian, he is Horus the Originator original Father or spirit.

The Senior Warden represents the setting sun, Shiva the destroyer or transmuter, for ever whose caste mark is a horizontal line, the Senior Warden's jewel. The Junior Warden is the sun at the Meridian the sunny side. He is Vishnu, the preserver during life and is associated with water and corn whose caste mark is a perpendicular line, mentioned in the olden days as representing falling rain the jewel of the Junior Warden. The upright line represents rectitude, which pulls to right and left the presses and represses of life it being our duty to keep this line perfectly erect. These three principal officers must act together in all Degrees if any progress is to take place in our work.

The Senior and Junior Deacons are still the messengers and the Inner Guard, under the control of the Junior Warden, the connecting link with the outer Guard; the world of the spirit (the Lodge) with the outside material world.

So we are in the world of the spirit, on a higher plane where the intellectual faculties are to be paramount and these seven officers will carry the candidate up to this level, working together to that end.

Who Comes Here?

A Brother who has taken his first step in Masonry, out of the darkness towards the light, from dim instinct into dawning insight, from the chaos of the senses into the ordered beauty of moral law; spiritual relations and righteous purpose; a seeker who has found in the Lodge the ground plan of a Temple, vast and slowly rising, whereon he would be a builder, making his life a living stone, shaped and polished by the Master of all good work; an Apprentice in the knowledge of God and the service of man, who fain would be a just and upright man.

What Came You Here To Do?

To discover myself, and how to rule and use the strange powers within my nature; to improve myself in the art of Masonry, by which the Rough Ashlar of youth is wrought into the Perfect Ashlar of manhood, noble and try; to learn to live with love and care.

Advancing by Regular Steps on the Square.

According to the old books and pictures, the black and white chequered pavement when laid in a church or cathedral symbolised the eternity of the world; in contrast to which a man, as he walked across the earth, was very humble and transient. Midway is the period of life when the soul passes through the ordeal of its Second Degree.

Nevertheless it is then if ever that a man becomes a man, worthy in the eyes of God to be entrusted with responsibilities; for, as the beautiful lesson of our Fellowcraft Degree has it, there is a Middle Chamber to be entered after one has climbed the wearisome winding stairs.

It is with certain satisfaction and joy that we find these signs or symbols which point out the right road to travel and mark our moral and spiritual progress much the same as the signs along the road marked out the pilgrims' progress in olden times; a hieroglyph moral system taught in ancient times by emblems and allegorical figures and having the four great ideas a belief in one God, a life after death, a symbolical idea of building a glorious spiritual Temple, and the task of seeking after something which was lost.

For our work in times borders on eternity. To study the sublime doctrine taught in the olden times by the virtuous and the great and to learn to walk in their shining footsteps. Such is he about to do. He has to pass the test of the questions, a review of his first entry Where, How, When, What and the Perfect Points of his Entrance.

Of, At and On.

In the olden days he was required to repeat his Obligation and to answer as many as 70 questions. In an old ritual the Master in opening a Lodge asks of the Junior Warden: 'How do you demonstrate the proof of your being a Freemason to others?'

Our Brother knows of the left hand pillar of 'Space and Creation' and has now passed between the two, learning of the right hand pillar of 'Time and Regeneration' on to the 'Path of Life'. The construction of these two pillars you know so well from the Tracing Board and the description of them in the talk on the Ceremony of Initiation, being the signs of 'Establishing for Ever'. No mortal can pass this way but through them. We can be happy that we know of them and can appreciate the landmarks of our Order and the meaning of progression in company with a great Brotherhood.

In the beautiful *Papyrus of Ani*, the original of which is in the British Museum, we find at the entrance of the Temple, two pillars dedicated to Horus and Set, the Gods of alternating light and darkness, bearing two spheres representing the terrestrial and celestial globes, of earth and heaven. These pillars were placed at the Gateway of the Higher World, the one being called *Tat*, which means in Egyptian 'Strength' and the other *Tattu*, which means 'The Place of Establishing for Ever'. According to the old Egyptian rites, these Temples were simply the earthly counterpart of Amenti, or heaven, and the Gates of Tattu led to the immortal region where the soul is established forever, as a dweller among the great ones in heaven, the teaching and ceremonies but illustrating the trials to which the spirit is subject until the journey to the 'throne of Glory' is accomplished.

You will remember they were cast on the clay ground between Succoth and Zeredatha. It is about 35 miles N.E. of Jerusalem. The clay there is of great tenacity, peculiarly fitted for making moulds.

Ears of corn were always buried with the deceased in the Egyptian rituals of the Dead symbolising Eternity, as they never die. I believe some ears of corn were taken from the jars filled with corn in Tutankhamun's Tomb and were planted and gave more ears, which were of a strong variety, large and of very good stock. Corn in the Indian ritual is said to be a 'Sacred Plant'. It never dies, however cut down, and always reasserts itself and comes again more vigorously than ever.

The ear of corn to a candidate is a symbol of his own growth, nourished by the living waters of knowledge from above. 'The righteous Man is as a tree planted by the waterside' (*Psalm 1:3*). Finally, Full C in the E. is exhibited in gold embroidery on the full dress collars of Grand Officers an emblem that what was once sown in them as bare grain has ripened to full knowledge.

In the Netherlands ritual, the ceremony is much more elaborate than ours. The candidate enters the Lodge veiled. Halfway through the ceremony, the veil is lifted and his attention is drawn to the Flaming Star and the Letter G. He is asked if he has now attained sufficient self-knowledge. He has to make five journeys: the first with the chisel and common gavel; the second with compasses and ruler; the third with ruler and level, the fourth with ruler and square, and finally, on the fifth, with no tool. The catechism consists of 28 questions and then the sign and word are given.

The left arm is to be supported in the angle of a Sq. The Lodge has ascended from the material to the spiritual and he enters on the square and asks for advancement.

In Ireland, the cable tow is wound round the candidate's neck; in the First Degree three times; in the Second twice; and in the Third once a gradual freeing from the 'darkness of understanding'.

The knocks of the Second Degree indicate symbolically that the physical work is complete and that the Fellowcraft has still two planes to conquer. He is now to make his astral body into a perfect instrument for the higher emotion of the final Degree.

Remembering that he originally came to the Lodge, urged to do so 'humbly soliciting', he is now 'recommended', having the assistance of the square and the benefit of the Pass Grip and Password.

In the first Prayer, 'Vouchsafe Thine Aid'; in the second, 'Supplicate the continuance of Thine Aid'. In the First; 'Begun in Thy Name'; in the Second; 'Continued to Thy Glory'. Progression. Our prayers, begun, continued and ended in Thee make it clear, as they are intended so to do, that the process of becoming a Master Mason is a *work* not merely a Ceremony.

It is appropriate that the Junior Warden, representing as he once did the Entered Apprentice Degree, should examine him as to his proof in the Degree and when he has passed his Gate he should then proceed to the Senior Warden in charge of a Fellowcraft Lodge and there he has to gain admittance, having passed through as Entered Apprentice Lodge, into the Fellowcraft lodge by giving the Password which will let him through that Gate and he is then presented to the WM as a Candidate ready to be Passed. He then passes along the North and enters the Lodge of a Fellowcraft.

We now have the perambulations as before in the 'Course of the Sun', in which he demonstrates to the Brethren that he is ready. And finally he makes his way to the East. Having learned to walk on the level, he comes to the central feature of the Degree. The winding staircase, full of symbolic meaning, twofold in character, vested with divine and human significance. The various steps of the different flights are typical of divine attributes of elemental expressions of Divine Creation and of the various forms of life on which that creative power has manifested itself. They also symbolise the various human faculties, the senses, wherewith knowledge is built up, and the Liberal Arts and Sciences. The cardinal idea of this Degree is essentially progress towards the knowledge the deeper understanding of himself, by study, by ruling his life, by entering into the interpretation of our hidden mysteries, by establishing strength in knowledge and by an increasing belief in the stability of our philosophy so that he will be enabled to pass into sovereignty of the greatest kingdom ever swayed by mortal hands the mastery of himself.

The penalty is again a most ancient one of the East, deeply feared by the oldest races. In the Ritual of the Dead when the deceased is passing his various trials it is rather significant that we find that among the prayers said for his are these: 'Let not my tongue be torn out...' and 'Let not my breast be laid open and my heart be torn away from me...' expressing, perhaps, two of the fears he had encountered in life as 'penalties which might be executed upon him in certain events'.

The position of the square and compasses is altered to indicate to him that spiritual principle is corning into activity within him and that he is now midway in Masonry. Immediately the Obligation is sealed our secrets are shared. He takes the second step; the second of the Three Taus. Our signs are acts of worship and promises.

The Sign of Fidelity implies not merely fidelity to his oath but obedience to the rules of TGGOTU, by which we can hope to be preserved only if we conform to those Rules laid down by Him for our preservation.

The Hailing Sign is said in our ritual to be the Sign of Perseverance; as old as when Shiva, the God Preserver, used it. The older Rituals give it as the Sign of Prayer; perseverance in prayer. The word... Man-plus-God. In the First, 'A Prince and Ruler' material and in the Second 'An Assistant High Priest' spiritual.

For God's House is Man and the Building of Man from quarry state of unconditioned Nature into strongly individualised living stone, perfect in all its parts and redounding in honour to the Builder, is the whole aim of our great Craft.

So the secrets of the Fellowcraft suggest he endeavours to examine and lay bare his heart, to cast away impurities from it, standing like Joshua, praying that the light of day may be extended to him until he has accomplished the overthrow of his own inward enemies and removed every obstacle to his further progress, so that he stands ready with confidence for that last and greatest trial by which he can enter into the great consolations and make acquaintance with the supreme realities of existence.

This sign is found among the Pathans, Dervishes, the Brahmins of India, the Central African Tribesmen, the Amsu a form of Risen God. Horus, in Ancient Egypt, is generally represented as having this sign, he is known as 'He who lifteth up his arm'. This God is the Spirit of the Sprouting Corn.

He passes the repeated trials to make sure that as he treads the path, his steps are true and the sign of progress is sure.

The illustration on the reverse of the frontispiece shows the salute to the new Pharaoh. In the Egyptian rituals are the words: 'I come from between the pillars, I had trodden the narrow way of the square and balanced good and evil in myself.'

He is invested with the badge of the Freemason. Still the white lambskin of innocence, but with two blue rosettes, one on each of the lower corners, indicating that the spiritual has now descended and is taking charge of the lower sign which is man; the triangle lowered to signify that advance; spirit and body working together with understanding. One old ritual says 'This down-pouring of the triangle typifies the now of the spirit into the square of Man.'

The two Rosettes are hieroglyphics of *light*; wisdom, forming the base, incomplete at present. When complete, the triangle of the spirit will be evident.

So a FC's apron is of a threefold nature, indicating the ascension of matter, the penetration of mind and the diffusion of the spiritual forces. The First Degree, Birth; the Second Degree, Life.

The rose symbol is one that pertains to the quest for God from the beginning of the path. The cathedral builders carved the rose symbol on the stonework with exquisite perfection.

He is placed in the South-East, his feet in the form of a square and maybe the perfect ashlar is placed in the right angle of his feet. He is expected to extend his researches. It is the practice of the author's Lodge to place the perfect ashlar in the right angle of his feet well and truly laid.

The Working Tools are now presented. In the First Degree, they were tools of *action*; the rough ashlar state is deemed to have given way to the condition symbolised by the perfect cube. In this Degree they are tools of *testing, trying, adjusting* and *proving* the square; justice and morality.

The level is the symbol of equality on which all men naturally stand in the sight of TGGOTU, advancing alike towards the end, subject to the same temptations, dangers and woes-partakers of the same hopes and fears. In some rituals as 'That vast Level of Time on which all men are travelling to its limits in Eternity'. It teaches humility.

The plumb rule is used to construct a Temple free from danger of falling. This can only be done by just and upright conduct, and is the symbol of rectitude – integrity.

The ancients seem soon to have discovered the principle of gravitation and the line of gravity in the plumb-line. The sun's outline provided them with the symbol of the eternal. It is round the tools of this Degree that the theory of Freemasonry is to some extent built. They are the everlasting tests; the triangle, the sign of the Divine, of the Trinity. There is the square at the base of the 3-4-5 triangle. From it, the circle, sometimes found alone but more often with the formative square; all these signs and symbols were found at the most unlikely places and found to originate in all the far-distant ages of the world's history, from a common ideal and for a common purpose. They also speak the common language of human religion and of human dependence upon the law of the almighty Lord. The square also is, among the emblems, most startlingly in evidence. It is referred to as the principle of Law by which all life should be regulated, and is evidenced by the picture language of every race which has built up anything at all.

To 'Live by the Square' meant, at all times that the law of uprights and perpendiculars alone could guide the art of mankind, whether in regard to the operative Craft or to that of the building of man.

The square stone formed the altar. The tools and symbols of the Mason are applied to the speculative field. The V.S.L. abounds with instances in which the symbology of the builder's art is used for the expression of thoughts affecting the life and character of mankind.

In the old Egyptian Ritual of the Dead, amulets were placed with the body of the deceased as a protection on the journey into the unknown and as proof of the fact that he had been possessed of virtues during his life. Thus we find the square placed upon the breast, a symbol of plenty and virtue; and the plummet to secure justice and moderation for the deceased in his coming trials.

He is instructed in the seven gifts of the spirit: wisdom, understanding, counsel, ghostly strength, knowledge, true godliness and holy fear of the seven corporeal works of mercy, and is reminded of the seven deadly sins: pride, envy, avarice, gluttony, lust, anger and sloth.

The seven periods of creation. The five Orders of Architecture and the five senses.

The Zodiac is a belt, 16 degrees wide, extending round the sky and having in its middle line the Great Circle (The Ecliptic) along which the sun appears to travel during the year. The marking off in the sky of the Zodiac, and the division of the belt into twelve equal parts, each named after a leading constellation in it, was the beginning of astronomy. This division is very old and was known to the Babylonians nearly 5,000 years ago. The visible heavens are the symbol of this Great Universal principle of life towards which all aspirations, all poetry and philosophy point as their highest goal, being the emblem of the universal, spiritual and eternal spirit. 'The heavens declare the glory of God, the firmament showed His handiwork'; day after day uttered speech, night after night sheweth knowledge. How true to our Brother these words are meant to be.

In the oldest of our institutions, this great belt is said to symbolise universalisation. Just as the heavens cover the universe so will Masonry cover the Earth in a great Brotherhood. TGGOTU, having no material form, exists, pervading all space, the creator of all things, governor of all animate and inanimate nature, the foundation of wisdom, whose greatness, perfection and glory is incomprehensible and whose loving-kindness and tender mercies are over all His other works.

In some districts, in the older Operative days, the Fellowcrafts were known as the Geometric Masons, and in those days the candidate was taught the theory of the 3, 4 and 5 rods.

The old name for the Second Degree was that of 'The 3, 4, 5'. Upon a right use of these rods depended many a jealously guarded secret, still preserved by the Guilds. Plutarch says in Egypt the Three Rods were dedicated to Isis, Osiris and Horus and each had a special colour: black, red and blue. By placing these rods together you get a right-angled triangle with sides 3, 4, 5 and the contents of which measure 6.

Vitruvius, a Roman Architect in possession of the secrets, wrote a treatise on Architecture about 25 BC, dedicated to Augustus Caesar. In *Ch. II, Book IX*, he says: 'Pythagoras demonstrated the method of forming a right-angle by rods,' and he then goes on to show how the square, which is described upon the sides subtending the right angle is equal to the square described upon the sides which contain the right angle and in his words; when Pythagoras discovered this properly, convinced that the Muses had assisted him in the discover, he evinced his gratitude to them by sacrifice.

Let us here recall the steps of the First, which are 9, 12 and 15; and let us consider the significance of these numbers. First developing them by squaring them and then balancing them by adding the squares of the first two together; when the sum will be found equal to the square of 15. We have here one of the most guarded secrets of the olden times.

Brethren, we now come to the climax to which the Degree has been progressing. The WM asks a question of the Junior Warden: 'What have you been enabled to discover In this Degree?' And the answer is, 'The Sacred Symbol.' 'Where?' 'In the E of the b.' 'To Whom does it allude?' 'To G; TGGOTU.'

So our Brother Fellowcraft is enabled to discover in the Middle Chamber the vital and immortal principle. The Lord of Life, which is found in the centre of each of us. By this is meant that the Brother has, in reality, advanced to the Second Degree in self-development. He has discerned that God is not outside him, but within him, overshadowing his own building, and that the rays of heaven will fill all the corners of his Being with Divine Wisdom. It is when the sacred symbol is discovered that we hear those lovely words: 'Brethren: Let us remember that wherever we are, whatever we do, his All-seeing Eye beholds us.'

The sacred symbol gives us a fuller conception of God than the symbol of the previous Degree, just as the idea of the Grand Geometrician transcends that of the Great Architect of the First Degree. The dormer window is symbolical of the light entering into the Temple of Man. How aptly was chosen the name of our own circle; that knowledge entering into him; so that seeing and hearing may be blended in him and his inner eye of the heart may instantly perceive, As Moses has said, 'I see Thy word O God.' Our Brother is a good way on the Path to becoming the Risen Master of the final Degree, the inevitable destiny to become perfected. He becomes 'a Dweller on the Threshold'.

Is this not a wonderful experience, sublime in its simplicity, great in its teaching and glorious to behold? In this short ceremony, the great things of life have been touched upon, a course set which will bring a thoughtful Brother much happiness in discovering the terms of the duties he owes to God, to Himself and to his neighbour. To render himself a fit and proper candidate for that which is to come and a life-long task elevating in its teaching, serene in its contemplation.

So, Brethren, 'In the meanwhile let us conduct ourselves in our several stations with honour to the Craft and credit to ourselves. Happy have we met; happy have we been; happy may we part and happy meet again.' We leave our Brother on the Path which will bring him to the 'Great Light', into the 'Hall of Wisdom'.

Chapter 6
Symbolism of the
Past Master's Jewel

Symbols are older than the written word; indeed, in all probability, the first gleams of intelligence in primal man were speedily followed by the invention of the symbol.

The usages and customs among Freemasons have ever borne a near affinity to those of the ancient Egyptians; indeed, two great men who had much influence on early Freemasonry lived in Egypt. They were Mr Euclid and Mr Pythagoras. The authors of those times published their works by means of hieroglyphics, or inscriptions, on stone; and the mason was the compositor of antiquity. They are quite safe from violation by virtue of the fact that they are capable of being fully understood only by those minds that have become sufficiently pure and spiritualised to apprehend and interpret them. They are universal and ageless and are to be found in all religions, philosophical systems and mythologies of whatever time or place in the world. Archaeologists continue to uncover more ancient cities and discover traces of extinct civilisations, and, in every discovery, they find these very same Masonic marks, signs and symbols engraved or carved on temples, palaces etc., thereby proving that they must have had the same meaning for all peoples for which they were delineated.

Our symbols, rituals and ceremonies portray the Drama of the Soul and indicate the obligatory Path to Perfection which has to be trod by every human soul.

The principal stages of our journey are marked by the Degrees. The First Degree is that of catharsis or purification, its symbol being the rough ashlar hewn from the quarry or universal substance as most of us are at this stage.

The Second Degree develops the moral and intellectual faculties and is depicted by the perfect ashlar, which has been shaped by working tools.

In the Third Degree is undergone that figurative death of the lower mortal man or the personality, then and only then can the Soul be raised as the higher immortal man, the individuality or spiritual ego. St Pauls says, (I Corinthians 15:42) 'There is a natural body and there is a spiritual body; it is sown in corruption, it is raised in incorruption.' The Indian Brahmins speak of the "Twice-Born", the Egyptians spoke of the 'Osirified Man'. The soul of man is a 'Living Stone' and is only then fitted to be built into that great Temple of Perfect Humanity, otherwise known as the Temple of God.

The means of overcoming obstacles on this Path to Perfection by transmuting selfish and material interests into altruistic and spiritual attributes are likewise laid down for our instruction in the Masonic ritual, by means of the working tools and proper instruments.

In the Charge after Initiation all candidates are adjured to make a daily advancement in Masonic knowledge. This knowledge is obtained not only by deep study but by right thoughts and actions, as Freemasonry is a way of life; it is the oldest and newest of all cults. It was in strength before the dawn of history and still rejoices in the vigour and glow of youth, enabling us to acquire wisdom and receive Divine Grace. Such, however, is the destiny possible to every human soul.

So that you may appreciate this preamble in more detail, I have selected one particular symbol which we see worn at all Lodge meetings; this is the Past Master's Jewel, presented to every Master of a Lodge after he has completed his year of office.

This symbol is a Master's square, with the 47th Proposition of Euclid appended to it and placed in a frame, adorned by ears of corn. The ear of corn itself is a symbol of the soul.

There is a close and intimate connection between the Elements of Euclid and our ritual. The Freemasons of some 3,000 years ago made use of these elements as a sort of manual, turning the various symbols, lines, angles, squares, circles and even solids into illustrations of moral ideas; and, as a consequence of this, much of what we do in our ceremonies today may be traced back to that remote antiquity.

We have all dabbled in Euclid at some time during our school days; no doubt many of us asked our tutor whether the problems might be made a little easier? Well, Brethren, the answer is 'There is no royal road to Geometry.'

There are two main facts which I ask you to observe: firstly, that the language of our Masonic ritual is very frequently the language of Euclid; and, secondly, that if we compare the two works, we will find many points of contact and many coincidences (Euclid's 47th Proposition etc.)

Euclid's 47th Proposition demonstrates that proof in every right-angled triangle, the square on the hypotenuse is equal to the sum of the squares on the other two sides. The measurements of the sides of the triangle in the Past Master's Jewel are the traditional 3-4-5; and the lines of the proof are shown on the completed symbol. We will first investigate the practical side of this symbol and afterwards we will define its Spiritual meaning.

From lines, we come to figures to lay lines and draw designs:

The method of describing an equilateral triangle on a given finite straight line is very simple. The two extremities of the line are used as the centres of the two circles, so that the line becomes the common radius. These two circles cut each other at their respective centres, and also at two points of the

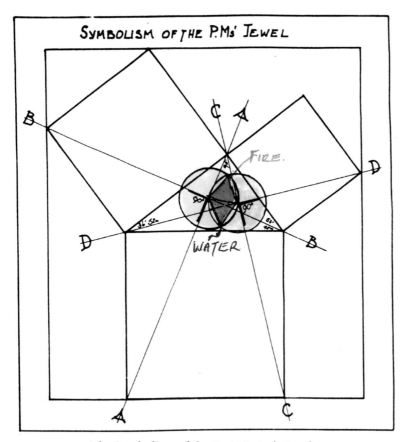

The Symbolism of the Past Master's Jewel

circumference. Now, any of three of those four points of intersection may be used to describe the required triangle; but described above the line it points up, while that described below the line points down. This is a simple geometrical problem, but it is capable of a mystic interpretation. We may therefore use it as exemplifying the method of our Ancient Brethren.

The given finite line was taken to represent human life. The two circles pointed to the fact that we belong to two worlds, and the two possible triangles showed that we may build in two different directions, according as we chose to work for purely material ends or for something better.

Again, the two triangles correspond to those which are suggested by the K.K.K. on the door on the Lodge in the Second and Third Degrees.

The Three Ks persist all through the ceremonies of Craft Masonry, but in the Second and Third Degrees are given differently: in an FC Lodge, we get K.KK., in an MM Lodge we get KK.K; the effect of the former is a triangle which points up, whilst the effect of the latter is one which points downwards; while two such triangles when interlaced produce the sacred symbols which the FCs report having discovered in the centre of the building (namely Solomon's Seal).

In ancient times it was customary in the Lodges of Operative Masons to have the craftsmen arranged in two straight lines, meeting at a right angle; and the Master used to take his place at the angle so as to be in view of all. The Lodge was thus opened on the Square.

One of the prime secrets of Operative Guild Masonry was that the Master of a Lodge carried a rod, measuring three units; the Senior Warden carried a similar rod, measuring four units; and the Junior Warden carried a rod, measuring five units. When these rods were joined together by the Master and the two Wardens they formed a right-angle triangle. In fact, the design of the speculative Past Master's Jewel is evidently derived from the knowledge of the Three Rods and of their uses; knowledge of the fact that the square on the side which subtends the right angle is equal to the sum of the squares on the other two sides. The oblong round the Proposition is obviously the Master's oblong, made by the union of the four squares.

It is now also clear what our Master H A meant when he said that 'without the consent and co-operation of the other two, he neither could, nor would, disclose the secret entrusted to him'. This, Brethren, is literally true; the Master with one rod could not make the triangle; he required the presence and assistance of the other two. When a Temple or public building was about to be constructed, the King or Ruler laid the centre stone with the proper ceremony, and with a chisel made the centre-dot on the stone, remarking, 'There is the centre of the building, work ye to it.'

These buildings were usually constructed in one of three forms: square; oblong 2-1; oblong 3-1. If a square building was to be constructed (as in the case of a Pyramid) the King decided on the size and he gave the distance, measured from the centre to each of the four corners. The length of the sides followed as a matter of course, but it was not considered in the setting out, which was simply based on the centre and the four corner points.

The three MMs, by means of their 3-4-5 rods, would form four right-angle triangles from the centre, and then place pegs to mark the corners; in the event that these pegs might be moved or disturbed, the ancient Masons, as long ago as the days of Babylon, adopted land-marks. They were quick to appreciate that if these pegs were moved, the building would be out of true and the whole setting-out process would have to be repeated. Therefore they adopted land-lines, which extended beyond the actual size of the intended structure.

It was the duty of every guild Mason to take great care that these ancient land-marks of the Order were carefully preserved; in fact, in the days of King Solomon, it was death to move a Freemason's land-mark or land-line.

Note that in the case of a square building, the four angles must each measure 90 degrees, or the fourth part of a circle. In the case of oblong buildings built to the proportion 2-1, the ancient Mason used the same five-point system, but the angle between the diagonal lines at the centre of the building having its length equal to twice its width is 53 degrees 07 minutes and the 53 degrees 07 minutes of the Master's square was used for this purpose. These ancient temples were constructed with the main hall or nave three times as long as its width, or in a proportion of 3-1; and its height was half the length. The 36 degrees 52 minutes angle of the Master's square was used in this instance. Such is the practical use of the Master's square made by our ancient Brethren in those days of long ago.

The introductory address to the First Lecture begins: 'Brethren, Masonry, according to the general acceptance of the term, is an art founded on the principles of Geometry and directed to the service and convenience of mankind. But Freemasonry, embracing a wider range and having a more noble object in view, namely the cultivation and improvement of the human mind, may with more propriety, be called a science, although its lessons for the most part are veiled in allegory and illustrated by symbols; inasmuch as, veiling itself under the terms of the former, inculcates principles of the purest morality.' We should understand the word 'morality' in the sense of the old morality plays which conveyed spiritual teachings, rather than confine its meaning to refer only to customs and ethics, although these too are very importance and necessary. In Proverbs 4:7, we read 'Wisdom is the principal thing; therefore get Wisdom and with thy getting get understanding.'

Pythagoras (c.570-495 BC), the meaning of whose name is 'Father Teacher', says, 'God geometrises.' Pythagoras was an outstanding figure in an age of great men – Zoroaster (c.630-550 BC), Confucius (551-479 BC) and Buddha (c.563-483 BC) were his contemporaries. It was an age of profound interest to the Craft; in the year 531 BC, according to tradition, the Third or G&R Lodge was opened at Jerusalem.

Now to interpret the spiritual meaning of our symbol: the 47th Proposition of the First Book of Euclid, the Jewel of a Past Master. The side of the triangle which measures three units represents Spirit, the Supreme Triad; the side measuring four units represents matter, the lower quaternary; and, if the conjoining angle is a right angle, the hypotenuse measures five units, representing self-conscious Man.

Man as a composite being comprises seven principles. The right angle represents the equal balance of spiritual and physical forces, so that neither shall bring detriment to the other. The perpendicular stands for the spiritual. The horizontal or physical conditions lie continually along the same plane, never rising above it nor falling below it; for should it do one or the other, it ceases to be perfectly physical. The perpendicular rising out of the physical plane at every point of its progress is constantly changing its position, growing upward and out of the physical environment beneath which it does not penetrate: it meets the physical at the point of contact only. The hypotenuse represents the bond of union which connects the physical and spiritual on the opposite ends of the line, the extreme points of the perpendicular and the horizontal coalescing with the extreme points of the hypotenuse, representing body, soul and spirit which are but manifestations of the Divine power and presence. Saint Paul says: 'Be ye therefore perfect even as your Father which in heaven is perfect.'

A square is a symbol of perfection. It has four equal sides and four equal angles of 90 degrees. This makes four equal perfection: 360 degrees or a whole circle. That which is perfect must be real and the real must be the Infinite Perfect One. The perfect supreme intelligence is represented by the square on the hypotenuse. The square, described on the perpendicular, shows forth the *perfect spirit*; while on the horizontal stands for the *perfect physical*. Because manifestation exists as physical, it does not follow that it is imperfect. Consequently, the square on the hypotenuse or Divine Perfect is equal to both the manifestations of *itself*: the perfect spiritual and the perfect physical. Not until they return into itself will their equality, each to each, be manifest.

I hope that this explanation will enable you to have some appreciation of the inestimable knowledge that is epitomised in the priceless jewels in the chalice of Freemasonry. The mystery of man, the mystery of the universe and the true understanding of man's relationship with God are concealed therein.

A veritable feast of wisdom is placed before us and it is entirely up to each of us, Brethren, how much he will partake of the Divine repast. May you find an ever-increasing and deepening interest in following our ritual and quietly contemplating the jewels throughout the unfolding of the Degrees during our ceremonies.

CHAPTER 7
The Most Ancient Lodge and Temple

The question of which Lodge is the oldest is a thorny one. Part of the problem is due to the strong oral tradition from which Lodge Mother Kilwinning No 0 claims evidence for the Lodge's existence from the time of the building of the abbey there. This was founded by Tironensian Monks *circa* AD1150.

Orthodox historians now demand more exacting evidence than simple oral tradition, and in this respect, the earliest evidence of a Scottish Lodge which still exists comes from the minutes of the Lodge of Edinburgh (Mary's Chapel) No 1. These minutes commence in July 1599 and are still in the possession of that Lodge.

The oldest Lodge records in the world are those of Lodge Aitchison's Haven which commence in January 1598. These minutes are now the property of the Grand Lodge of Scotland.

Lodge Canongate Kilwinning No 2 received its Charter from Mother Kilwinning No 0 in 1677. The present Lodge rooms were built in 1736. In 1739 the Lodge paid for a piece of ground on which the Lodge rooms were built. As far as is known, this is the oldest Lodge room in the world still in use.

The mutual contract of 1658 by the Masons of Scone and Perth is still in existence, and for several reasons is very important, not least because it is the first Masonic document to mention King Solomon's Temple. It also claims that King James I became a Freemason in that Lodge.

The Schaw Statutes of 1598 and 1599, of which several are still extant, are of paramount importance to Freemasonry, for William Schaw may be considered to be the father of modern Freemasonry. It is impossible within the compass of a few pages to do more than trace, in outline, the rise and progress of these venerable old Lodges.

The study of Freemasonry in Scotland involves a return to medieval times as the development via the Mason Word followed lines very different from those of England. Then, though material is very plentiful, it is less easily digested. Scotland is rich in records of both the operative and the pre-Grand Lodge speculative Craft.

Mother Kilwinning is a name as hallowed in Scotland as is York to England. The town of Kilwinning, once only a village, is one of great age and lies in the county of Ayrshire on the west coast of Scotland. The Abbey of Kilwinning was founded in 1140 and dedicated to St Winning. Dr. Mackey, in his *Lexicon of Freemasonry*, says, 'The little village of Kilwinning was the birthplace of

Freemasonry' and, in an old parchment writing of 1658, the Lodge of Scoon and Perth No 3 declares that 'the Kilwinning Temple of Free Masons was the Temple which was first instituted in Scotland'. It is one of the oldest traditions of Scotland that the Provincial Grand Master of Ayrshire becomes ipso facto the RWM of Mother Kilwinning Lodge No 0. The colours of the Lodge are green and gold, which were adopted as the official ones of the Grand Lodge of Scotland after it was constituted in the most ancient Lodge room in the world – that of St. John's Chapel of Lodge Canongate Kilwinning No 2, Edinburgh.

In those ancient days it was not the custom for Masons' Lodges or Societies, Operative or Speculative, to make official notes, 'minutes', or similar entries of their work or proceeding. People who have never belonged to, or even visited, the most ancient Lodges as Lodges, and not trade societies for some of the latter would have us believe they were Lodges long before they were or examined *in situ* their old historical and traditional claims, have no right whatever to assume authority and say that such bodies did not exist, do what they did, and have no justification whatever for their world-renowned fame, just because there happens to be very little or, according to their prejudiced ideas, no written paraphernalia of their remote proceedings still in existence.

In 1128, a number of Masons of and about Kilwinning responded to the call of King David I of Scotland, and journeyed south-east to Edinburgh to help build the Abbey and Palace of the Holyrood. In 1140, the Masons of Kilwinning began to restore their own abbey. At the top of the parchment certificate of membership, which is printed in green, are three circular pictures, surmounted by an interwoven circle and triangle (the emblems of heaven and earth) enclosing a capital letter G.

On 14th December 1658, a document known as a *Charter* was granted by Kilwinning to the Lodge of Scoon and Perth afterwards No 3 which gave the approximate date of the foundation of Lodge Kilwinning as 465 years before (1193). The old minute in fact recites that the Lodge proceeded from Kilwinning, the first Masonic Lodge established in Scotland in 1286, the Lodge was presided over by King James, who was the 'Lord Steward of Scotland', when two Free or Speculative Masons were admitted; one being an English Earl of Gloucester and the other an Irish one from Ulster. In 1311, King Robert the Bruce presided at the Lodge and, then and there, instituted the Masonic Order of Heredom de Kilwinning. He afterwards instituted the *Rose Croix* from Jerusalem. He presided over the Lodge again after the Battle of Bannockburn, which was fought on 24th June 1314. The Lodge was afterwards presided over by the third son of King Robert II. In 1491, King James IV 'held a Masonic Festival at Kilwinning'. It is amazing the pull this unique Lodge has on the imagination of Brethren in all parts of the world, and the increased respect and stability which the Craft enjoys in, and through, its wonderful past, and also in the fact of its existence at this very day. Its ramifications are worldwide, its work almost beyond belief and its standing unassailable.

At a Lodge meeting the Deputy Master was asked 'What Book do you use?' which seemed to momentarily dumbfound him. Recovering he said 'Book?' 'Yes' said the questioner, 'What Book?' The DM still astonished, asked 'Book? What Book? We don't use a Book, never have done. What you have heard here has been handed down to us by word of mouth.' Happily there is not any set book ritual in Scotland, nor in fact are there any Lodges of Instruction, nor any combination, who, by advertisement, claim impossible things that are better than everybody else, and only true shining exponents of Masonic ceremonies. If a Master of a Scottish Lodge has good reason to think he can enhance a ceremony by adding or taking away a few lines, then he is at liberty to do so, sometimes producing a wonderful bit of high-class Masonic oratory.

The most ancient Masonic building

The Lodge room is known as St John's Chapel, the front entrance to which is in St John Street, off the Canongate, Edinburgh. The door to which it leads opens onto a small entrance hall, formerly a store room or scullery, from which runs a winding staircase to the Lodge rooms and Chapel above. It is all very old and crowded. The author believes that the Chapel itself is the oldest Masonic Lodge room in the World, there is not the slightest doubt about that; it has for ages been a Lodge Room. It is the only Lodge in Edinburgh that has been dedicated to Freemasonry; nothing else has ever entered its sacred walls. The Lodge's traditions as an operative body begin with the building of Holyrood Abbey and Palace in 1128, for which purpose King David Iof Scotland called all the Masons together.

The Master's Chair dates back to about 1690.

The Secretary's Chair to about 1500.

The Master and Wardens form an equilateral triangle.

The Wardens' Jewels are believed to be the oldest in the kingdom.

The 'Lokkit Kist' is about 380 years old. More research is being carried out to find out exactly what this is!

The Grand Lodge of Scotland was formed under its roof, and its then-RWM was made the first Most Worshipful Grand Master Mason of Scotland.

One of the rooms of the building on the same first floor as the Chapel was long known as the 'old kitchen', which had formerly been reduced in size by a wall and partitions. These were later removed and opened up the old fireplace, the lintel of which bears the date of 1486, with the ancient motto: *The morw ne sorw be heir* 'The morrow, no sorrow be here' with the emblems of the Daisy, the Anchor and a Heart, representing Faith; Hope and Charity. This most ancient and venerable Lodge room has never been altered, for it is held too sacred to touch or enlarge, though more space is sadly needed for its wonderful work, being renowned for its ceremonial procedure and perfect accomplishment from time immemorial. Being in Edinburgh, the capital city, the Lodge is always the very centre of Freemasonry there, and it has taken into its membership many great and eminent men of all nations.

It would take one and a half hours to explore its wonderful museum and look through its many relics. There is a marble bust of Burns, and an annotated copy of the Qur'an on which Muslims are obligated on entering or affiliating.

The origin of this ancient Lodge is lost in the mists of time. The oldest extant minute of the Lodge is dated the last day of July 1599. It is a deliverance on a breach of the statute against the employment of 'Cowans' and is the oldest minute of any existing Lodge in the world.

A minute of 1600 records that the Lodge of Edinburgh met in Holyrood House. The first mention of Mary's Chapel in the minutes of the Lodge is on 25th November 1613. In this minute it is called *Maries Chaipill in Nidries Wynd*. This Chapel, built in 1504 by the Countess of Ross, was, in 1618, bought by the Incorporation of Wrights and Masons and was, by them, made their Convening House. The earliest extant Minute of any Lodge meeting in England is contained in the first Minute Book of the Lodge of Edinburgh, in which it is recorded that at Newcastle, on 20th May 1641, the Right Honourable Mr Robert Moray, General Quartermaster to the Army of Scotland, was admitted to membership of the Lodge. At that time, the Scottish Army, in which were several members of the Lodge of Edinburgh, was besieging Newcastle.

Lodge Canongate Kilwinning No 2
Brother Alexander McKenzie states, 'When an institution survives the vicissitudes of over two centuries, it becomes entitled to our veneration and respect.' Since these lines were penned in 1888, our country has experienced even greater and more devastating vicissitudes, and still the institution survives; and the institution will continue to survive because it is built on a solid foundation. The motto of Lodge Canongate Kilwinning is *Post Nubila Phoebus*, which may be interpreted 'After the Clouds, the Sun will shine'. From time immemorial the Lodge has never closed it is adjourned from one meeting to the next. At the conclusion of Lodge business, the Master instructs the Senior Warden 'to close the work, and adjourn the Lodge', and the last words of the Junior Warden are 'And the work is closed and the Lodge adjourned accordingly.' Although this may be regarded by some as simply traditional, it is fundamentally symbolic. The teachings within the Lodge do not cease to become effective when the Lodge is 'closed'- the Lodge is never 'closed', it is 'adjourned.' Behind the Master's chair in Canongate Kilwinning is a painting of the sun in its full splendour, with all its radiant Masonic symbolism; and,

again, our thoughts are directed to the continuity of our system by the words of one of our well-known Scottish hymns: 'The sun that bids us rest is waking, Our Brethren 'neath the Western Sky.'

The name of the Lodge is not simply Canongate but Canongate Kilwinning and this is significant. The operative Masons after the subsequent building of Holyrood House by Charles II but not until the year 1677 that the Canongate Masons expressed a wish to be associated with the parent body of Masons at Kilwinning in Ayrshire. It was to the Masons in these distant parts that a petition for a Charter was submitted. Canongate Kilwinning No 2 is very proud to be the eldest daughter of the Mother Lodge of Scotland, Mother Kilwinning No 0.

Interesting Dates
1588 Defeat of the Spanish Armada.
1598 (January) Oldest recorded Lodge Minutes – about 400 years old.
1603 Union of the Crowns of Scotland and England.
English Lodges before 1717:
Now No2 Lodge of Antiquity Time Immemorial.
Now No4 Royal Somerset House of Inverness. Time Immemorial.
Now No12 Lodge of Fortitude and Old Cumberland. Time Immemorial.
Old Meeting Houses in London:
The Goose and Gridiron Ale House, St Paul's Church Yard.
The Crown Ale House, Parker's Lane (off Drury Lane).
The Apple-Tree Tavern, Charles Street, Covent Garden.
The Rummer and Grapes Tavern, Chapel Row, Westminster.

I have actually visited Mother Kilwinning, both its Lodge and Chapter, and also St John's Chapel in Edinburgh, with its 'Old Kitchen'.

Remember always, that whilst Operative Masonry is engaged in the construction of edifices by means of stone, Speculative Masonry is a science which, borrowing from the Operative Art, its working tools, sanctifies them, by symbolic instruction to the Holiest of all purposes, the veneration of God, and the purification of the soul.

The Seal of Lodge
Mother Kilwinning

Acknowledgements
Masonic Lectures & Addresses by Bro A. Holmes-Dallimore, PM of Lodges in England; Scotland and Ireland.
The First Freemasons; Scotland's Early Lodges and their Members by David Stevenson.
Mother Lodge Kilwinning by Revd William Lee Ker, MA.
Bro C. Martin McGibbon; Grand Secretary Grand Lodge of Scotland.
Bro Ronnie Lubell, Masonic Historian.

CHAPTER 8

Glimpses of the Royal Arch Ritual and the Vault

The Royal Arch Degree is the *Pilgrim's Progress* of Freemasonry. It is the most widely known and talked about degree in the Masonic system. Why? Because it once climaxed the old system of symbolic Degrees; not as a separate Degree, but as part of the Third Degree.

The Royal Arch Degree was conferred in Craft Lodges under the sway of the Grand Lodge of the Ancients, and in 1756 Dermott described the Royal Arch as "the Root, Heart and Marrow of Masonry".

In those times the Royal Arch was confined to Past Masters, and probably was taken after preliminary qualifying Degrees such as Past Master of Arts and Sciences and Excellent Master had been conferred.

In England a MM may be exalted into the R.A., the ceremony taking place in a properly constituted Chapter.

In Scotland the Craft Mason *must* take the Mark and Excellent Master Degrees before he can become a R.A. Mason; he takes the Mark in a Craft Lodge or in a Chapter, and takes Excellent Master in a Chapter.

In Ireland the Craft Mason, before he can become a R.A. Mason, *must* take the Mark Degree and he can do this only in a R. A. Chapter.

Of the three countries, it is only in England that the Chapters are attached to a particular Lodge.

No one seems to know when R.A. Masonry was born or even the place of its origin. Some Masonic historians have endeavoured to locate its origin in France where degrees were once manufactured and sold by the hundreds, some of which still plague the world today. Others believe its birthplace as an organised Degree was England or Ireland; in fact the earliest actual reference to the degree is in the USA, where, on 22 December, 1753, the Degree of R.A. was conferred in the old Lodge at Fredericksburg, Virginia, for in those days this Degree, as well as others, was that which George Washington was initiated. The diffusion of R.A. Masonry among English Masons in the latter half of the 18th century owes much to the enthusiasm and exertions of Laurence Dermott and Thomas Dunkerley.

Dermott may be regarded as the father of R.A. Masonry. As far as existing records go, he did not invent the R.A., but he certainly did amplify it and propagate it. He claims to have been Exalted in Dublin on 4th March 1746, and was a prominent member of the Grand Lodge of the Ancients in which he served as Secretary and, later, as Deputy Grand Master for ten years.

There is much to learn about the early history of R.A. Masonry, much that remains conjecture, for very little is known of the degree before we find it suddenly rising in the Lodges of the 1740s-1750s as a new and separate rite.

Definitely the R.A. was worked in Ireland and probably Scotland in the 1740s. Minutes show the Irish and Americans to have worked the R.A. in the 1750s and there are many references as to leave no doubt that by the 1760s, rudimentary R.A. ceremonies were being worked throughout English, Irish, Scottish and American Freemasonry.

Anderson, in his *Constitutions* of 1723, refers to 'the Royal Arch being cultivated, and the cement of Brotherhood preserved', so that the whole body resembles a well-built arch.

Those same *Constitutions* granted to the Master of a Lodge, authority to congregate the members into a Chapter, and in 1723 on one occasion 'the Minutes of the last Chapter' of the Old King Arms Lodge No 28 were read to the satisfaction of 'the society present'. Whatever the word 'Chapter' meant to Anderson or was in the mind of the Secretary who wrote those minutes, it cannot be positively claimed that a Chapter of R.A. Masons was intended.

Thomas Dunkerley came prominently into the early history of the R.A., for, in a letter, he says he was made a R.A. Mason in 1754 (probably in an R.A. Lodge attached to his Mother Lodge in Portsmouth).

By some he has wrongly been credited with being the founder of R.A Masonry. He was not that, but he was one of the few who helped to keep Grand Chapter of the Moderns in working order.

It is possible that the oldest minutes of a Lodge connecting the Moderns with the R.A. refer to meetings at the Crown Inn, Christmas Street, Bristol, in 1758, a Lodge officially Modern but probably working the Ancient ritual. Its minutes of 7th August and Sunday, 13th 1758 leave us no doubt that two Brethren were 'raised' to the Degree of a Royal Arch.

In the 1760s, there grew out of the Punch Bowl Lodge at York, constituted in 1761, one of the earliest separate R.A. Lodges (1762). Its original members were all actors and members of the York Company of Comedians. One of them had been the first Master of the Punch Bowl Lodge. They were all men of Hull and it is thought likely that they had been made R.A. Masons in that city.

The Punch Bowl Lodge was the centre of much Masonic activity and was a factor in the revival of the York Grand Lodge. In 1768, the R.A. Lodge became a Chapter, in due course to become a Grand Chapter.

It would be a mistake to assume that the York Grand Chapter was the first of the Grand Chapters. The one instituted by the Moderns grew out of a Chapter associated with the Caledonian Lodge, London, which had been an Ancient Lodge constituted in 1763, but in 1764 the Brethren changed their allegiance and obtained a Charter from the Premier Grand Lodge as No 325, now No 134. In course of time came a Chapter in association with the Lodge, and in this Chapter Lord Blayney, Grand Master of the Moderns was exalted.

In June 1766, at a meeting at the Turks Head Tavern, Gerrard Street, Soho, London, 27 Companions witnessed the Exaltation of Lord Blayney, who was the first Grand Master of England to join the Royal Arch.

At the July meeting a month later, the famous Charter of Compact was drawn up; it constituted the Chapter in which Lord Blayney had been exalted to be the Grand and Royal Chapter of the Royal Arch of Jerusalem with full power to hold and convene Chapters, and to constitute, superintend and regulate others. It also designated Lord Blayney as the M.E. Grand Master of Royal Arch Masonry. During his two years as GM of the Craft he constituted 74 Lodges, of which 19 still exist.

Undoubtedly much of the work devolved upon his able lieutenant Thomas Dunkerley, who became Provincial Grand Master of Hampshire in 1767, later to become Prov GM of 8 other countries. In 1778, he became Grand Superintendent of the Royal Arch in Kent and, later still, he became Grand Superintendent in seventeen other countries. In this manifold capacity he became founder or sponsor for many Chapters and gave tremendous impetus to the spread of R.A. Masonry. Over a hundred Chapters had been warranted by the Grand Chapter at the time of Thomas Dunkerley's death in 1795.

The growth of Royal Arch Masonry thus promoted largely by the labours of Thomas Dunkerley was principally among Masons owing allegiance to the Premier Grand Lodge, and thus the way was paved for the Union of the Grand Lodges in 1813. Nevertheless the newly formed Grand Lodge, whilst maintaining no control over the Royal Arch Degree, set forth its status in the Masonic system by the following statement:

'It is declared and pronounced that pure ancient Masonry consists of three degrees and no more. Namely, those of the EA, the FC, and the MM, including the Supreme Order of the Holy Royal Arch.'

And today, in the Grand Lodge of England, we find the connection with the Grand Chapter of Royal Arch Masons so close that Grand Officers of the Grand Lodge, by virtue of their Grand Lodge station, often hold similar positions in Grand Chapter.

Examination of minutes of Craft Lodges of Instruction at the time of the Union shows that these old Lodges of Instruction formed to promote knowledge of Masonry among their members, who achieved their objecting by working the lectures rather than by rehearsing the ceremonies. These lectures in the form of question and answer – the catechetical form of instruction used from the remotest times – provide a commentary on the three Degrees and have been preserved by regular rehearsal. The test questions put to candidates before Passing and Raising are based on these lectures and the Master's reference to 'other questions' suggests that at one time the conductor of the candidate was expected to know the whole section of the relevant lecture.

In the same way, Aldersgate working in the R.A. has spread largely because the Aldersgate Chapter of Improvement has had the same plural governance that has maintained immutability in the ritual and ceremonial.

The Aldersgate Chapter No 1657 was formed in 1876, its Chapter consecrated in 1883 and the Chapter of Improvement established in 1900.

Its ritual was first printed in 1822. It is clear, therefore, that Aldersgate working must have been derived from some older working. Evidence based on a comparison of the ritual indicates that Aldersgate stemmed from Domatic working. The Domatic Lodge No 177 was founded in 1786, its Chapter constituted in 1793, some 90 years prior to the consecration of the Aldersgate Chapter.

From an old manuscript of the ritual written certainly before the 19th century we find that the three Principals alone were present at the opening and that it was not until they had opened the Chapter that Past Principals and Companions were admitted. At a later date, all Principals were allowed to be present, but it was not until 1902 that R.A. Companions below the rank of Principal were allowed to witness the full opening.

We have an explanation here of the variation of the words at the opening and closing, viz. 'We three d.m.a.a.' for opening and 'We all d.m.a.a.' for closing. This change in 1902 did not affect Grand Chapter, all of which are either actual or past Principals.

Despite the fact that it is *not now* necessary to have three candidates for an Exaltation, it is interesting to note a trace of the old custom in our present ritual. It is now a common occurrence to have one candidate only, but he is seldom addressed in the singular during the ceremony, and in the few instances where the singular is used, a reversion to the plural takes place shortly afterwards. An example of this is 'such, my newly exalted Companion, is the best explanation I can give', followed shortly afterwards by 'Companions, I charge you...' A failure to understand that in each case these words are addressed only to the newly exalted Companion is probably the reason why we occasionally see an E.Comp. when giving the Mystical Lecture, turn to all the Companions, in the Chapter, from the mistaken impression that the admonition is addressed to all Companions present. It will have been noticed that each of the three lectures commences with the word Companions, but those lectures are delivered directly to the candidates who have just passed through the ceremony of the Exaltation and not to all the Companions in the Chapter.

There is also a connection here with an old Regulation still existent in some jurisdictions that the number of candidates to be exalted at any one time must be three or groups of three, 'neither more nor less'. The three appear again in the old catechism.

'Are you a R.A. Mason?'   'I am that I am.'
'How shall I know you to be a R.A. Mason?'   'By three times three.'

The legend which forms a motif of the R.A. ritual is not everywhere the same, which rather points to the probability that if and when the substance of the original Degree came from the Continent, it arrived almost at the same time both in London and in Dublin, and in somewhat different forms.

The English R.A. adopted its legend the 'Rebuilding of the Temple', whereas the Irish based theirs on the 'Repairing of the Temple'.

The first of these legends is the narration of Ezra; the second of Josiah. In the English legend we have as the three chief officers Zerubbabel, Prince of the people; Haggai, the Prophet; and Joshua, the High Priest, whereas in the Irish legend the three officers or Principals are Josiah, the King; Hilkiah, the Priest; and Shaphan, the Scribe (see II Kings 23 & II Chronicles 34).

Scotland and America took the R.A. legend from England, but America borrowed the names of the Principals from Ireland, and is, therefore, working English legend but with Principals different in name from those that we know.

This is not to say that the American and Scottish systems are the same as the English; they are not, particularly the American, but the basic legend is the same.

Undoubtedly there has been incorporated within its ritual emblems, symbols and religious concepts from various parts of the world.

The equilateral triangle is one of the most ancient of symbols, and so sacred was the emblem regarded that in the days of Pythagoras when an obligation was to be administered it was invariably given on the triangle, and when so taken, no one was ever known to violate it.

The triangle was used by the alchemists in various ways: with the apex upward, it meant fire; with the apex downward, it meant water. Symbolically, the fire may be held to correspond to things spiritual, the water to things material, so that the combination in the interlaced triangles, the hexagram, represented a fusion of things temporal with things spiritual and it well applied to the teachings, tenets and principles of Royal Arch Masonry.

This integration is further exemplified at the opening and closing of every Chapter when the Principals make a triangle with their hands, on which the VSL is placed and another with their hands on the VSL, thus enfolding the spiritual with the material.

The interlaced triangles are usually inscribed with a circle which is an emblem of eternity, for as it has neither beginning nor end it may justly be deemed a type of God, without beginning of days or end of years.

Hebrew characters, thus:
Shelomoh Meleck Israel,
Huram Meleck Tsur,
Huram Ben Almanah

Author's Impression of the Vaulted Chamber Chamber Catenary: the curve formed by a flexible homogeneous cord such as a chain hanging freely between two points of support and acted on by no other force than gravity. N.B There is no such thing as a Catenarian Arch in Architecture.

The circle as an emblem of eternity dates from the ancient Egyptian papyri: the Ouroboros, or wreathed serpent, or snake coiled about a centre eating its own tail, is regularly featured.

Time will not permit me to go all through the Ceremony of Exaltation, but I will endeavour to try and answer one question so often put to me: 'what is a Catenarian Arch?'

Freemasonry knows the Arch as not only a symbol of strength but as a symbol of heaven

What the term 'Catenarian Arch' really means is that the arch has a curve the same as that assumed by a chain or heavy rope suspended between two points. The suspended chain assumes its own curve, and the curve inverted becomes the outline of an arch, *Catena* being Latin for chain.

The sojourners clearing the rubble discovered, obviously at almost floor level of the passage since the PS struck down at it, a *dome*. Having discovered this dome we hear no more of it, since we immediately begin to wrench forth Archstones and the Keystone.

A dome has no *keystone* but does possess a *boss* or centre stone, probably many sided.

They then descended and explored a vault which must have been below the underground passage. Now, if we can get over the difficulty of making an aperture without collapsing the whole dome, the object of the vault becomes clear since we recognise the great necessity of safe guarding its contents and its engravings.

The vaulted crypt that plays its great part in the legend is, of course, itself legendary, Freemasonry knows the arch not only as a symbol of strength but as a symbol of heaven.

The difficulty with the legend of the discovery of a vault in the Temple is, however, that there is not a vestige of corroboration in the VSL.

The compilers of the mystical legend have used the Hindu conception of the creative, preservative and destructive aspects of the deity Trimurti, who unites in One Person the creative aspect of Brahma, the preservative aspect of Vishnu, and the destructive character of Shiva.

Further, the double triangle within a circle is the emblem of Trimurti. The Point within a Circle, the symbol of the *deity* surrounded by *eternity*, is also a Hindu symbol denoting *Paramata*, the All-Pervading Supreme Being (the hexagram – 'G').

In Richard Carlile's *Manual of Freemasonry*, there are full accounts of the ceremony of Passing the Veils; a part of this ceremony is still observed in Bristol Working. In the American Working the PS reads *Exodus 3: 1-6* whilst the candidate is perambulated, and at the appropriate point the h-w was raised when he saw a representation of the Burning Bush. A hidden voice then called,

'Draw not nigh hither; put off thy shoes from thy feet; for thy place whereon thou standest is holy ground.' The candidate was then made to kneel and cover his face in reference to 'Moses hid his face'.

This Passing through the Veils can be regarded as an allegorical representation of man's journey from this world to the next; or was intended to represent the trials, tribulations and obstructions met with by the repatriated Jews in their journey from Babylon to Jerusalem.

The building of the Temple is described in great detail, but there is no hint whatever that Solomon had a vault constructed under it, or had the idea of hiding the Law of Moses etc. for future posterity. Nor is there any reference to such a vault by Josephus or other writer; at least no such record has come to light as yet. Likewise, there is no record in Ezra or Nehemiah of the discovery of any such vault at the rebuilding of the Temple, which was *circa* 450 BC. Neither Ezra nor Nehemiah refer to the matter, either the finding of a vault or the Book of the Law. In *II Kings 22*, there is, however, a record of the finding by Hilkiah, the High Priest, of 'the Book of the law in the House of the Lord'. There is no suggestion of any vault.

This putting away of the VSL occurred during the idolatrous reigns of previous Kings of Judah, and it was forgotten. On being found by Hilkiah among the archives it was read by Shaphan, the Scribe, to King Josiah, who at once set about putting down idolatry and reinstating the Law of the Lord. It is on this incident that the Irish ceremony (alone) of the Royal Arch is based.

All other R.A. rituals are based on the supposed finding of a vault in the ruins of the Temple. The story of Josiah and the Book of the Law does not account for the legend of a vault containing an altar of incense etc.

While, therefore, there is historical basis for the story adopted by the Irish R.A. Chapters, how are we to account for the legend of a vault containing an altar of incense, etc.? In Josiah's reign, this altar was still in the Temple of course: what happened to it?

The finding of a secret vault or cave is sometimes to the accompaniment of storms, fire or other manifestation. The stories range from that of King Gyges of Lydia, *circa* 600 BC who is alleged to have found a cave on his estate in which was a solid gold ring with magical properties, to that of the historian Philostorgius, *circa* AD 400, who describes the alleged finding of a cave hollowed out of rock underneath the Temple at Jerusalem, the ruins of which were being cleared away, and in which was a column or pillar on top of which was a copy of Saint John's Gospel.

The legend is that this cave or vault was constructed by King Solomon for the reception of a copy of the Word and Name of God; but as the Temple was built a thousand years before the time of Saint John, the story alleging the finding of his Gospel is an anachronism.

In the tradition as now given in our Chapters it is the Law of Moses which is found in the vault, together with an altar of incense and a P... of gold.

In many old ceremonies and still in use today in some workings are models of the Ark, the Tables of Stone, Aaron's Rod, the Pot of Manna, etc., or reference to them. And on many old aprons are delineated the Burning Bush, the Serpent, Aaron's Rod, the Ark, etc., showing that they were in regular use.

The principal features of the legend are a cave, an altar of incense and the Book of the Law. If now we turn to *II Maccabees 2: 4-7*, we shall find a possible answer to the problem. As some may not have access to the Apocrypha, I will quote the passage in full:

4.) It was also contained in the same writing, that the prophet (Jeremiah), being warned of God, commanded the tabernacle and the ark to go with him, as he went forth into the mountain, where Moses climbed up and saw the heritage of God.

5.) And when Jeremy came thither he found a hollow cave, wherein he laid the tabernacle and the ark, and the altar of incense, and so stopped the door.

6.) And some of those that followed him came to mark the way, but they could not find it.

7.) Which, when Jeremy perceived, he blamed them, saying, As for that place it shall be unknown until the time that God gather his people again together and receive them unto mercy.

This incident took place *circa* 583 BC, just prior to the sack of Jerusalem by Nebuchadnezzar, who transferred the rest of the Holy Vessels of the Temple to Babylon. These vessels were later restored under an edict of Cyrus, King of Persia, to the Jews at the rebuilding of the Temple under Ezra and Nehemiah. But the Ark etc. are without doubt still in the cave at Mount Nebo, where they were deposited by Jeremiah.

The story of this hiding of the principal treasures of the Temple is, of course, well known and accepted by Jewish writers, referred to by the famous Rabbi Juda Hallevi in an elegiac poem he wrote in AD 1140.

Some of you will remember that ancient copies of Isaiah and other works were discovered a few years ago in caves in the hills opposite Mount Nebo, on the west side of the Dead Sea.

The discovery of Jeremiah's cave will be an epoch-making event, but it is doubtful if the discovery will be made similarly to that of the Dead Sea Scrolls. More probably it will be found as a result of the great earthquake in the not very distance future, when Jerusalem will become a sea-port and the Nile will be diverted. But, as Rudyard Kipling said, this is another story.

It is clear from the record quote that some people knew that Jermiah had hidden some treasures in a cave on Mount Nebo, and guessed, if they did not know, they were Temple Treasures.

In fact, from the circumstances of the case and Jeremiah being a well-known authority in Judea, it is more than probable that this intention was known to many. The story of the hiding of the treasures would naturally be handed down to successive generations.

The Ark of the Covenant was 'a large chest' and contained the Tables of Stone, the Book of the Law, the pot of Manna, etc. It seems clear also, there, that the story of Jeremiah depositing all these things fully accounts for the legend incorporated in the R.A. ritual, and for the numerous references to the treasures in our rituals generally.

The Ark is a feature of the heraldic Arms of Grand Lodge; it used to be used or referred to in our rituals, and is still so used, notably in America.

In the library of the Grand Lodge of England is a copy of a privately printed small book, anonymous, entitled *Royal Arch Ritual*, dated 1874. In this ritual, the candidate, after passing the Veils, is shown the Ark of the Covenant, the Tables of Stone, the Pot of Manna, the Burning Incense, the Shewbread and the seven branch Candlestick.

In some Scottish Craft Rituals, the candidate, after the r..., is shown most of these things, together with the coffin (this I have seen).

Another legend is that there are several vaults under the site of King Solomon's Temple and one of them may have been under the Sanctum Sanctorum. Those of you who have visited Jerusalem and have been in the Mosque of Omar will have been taken where the spirits of deceased Moslems assemble twice a week for united prayer. But it seems much more probable that it was originally a drain to carry away the blood from the sacrifices offered on Mount Moriah which is immediately above this vault. Many Jews to this day believe, and in fact have told me, that under this cave will be found hidden, since the destruction of Jerusalem, the vessels of the Temple and the treasures of the Kings of Judah.

The Book of the Law discovered in the vault was not the Bible as thoughtlessly might be concluded. The Scroll of Sacred Writing was the Torah, itself a Hebrew word for 'Law', but used also to indicate the Pentateuch, 'Five Books', the first five books of the Old Testament. The Pentateuch is also referred to as the 'Law of Moses', 'The Book of Moses' or 'The Book of the Law and the Lord'.

Traditions usually, if not invariably, have some basis of truth in them, but they die very hard, though sometimes a bit distorted during the passing years, but the essentials have been preserved remarkably well, especially in the Bristol version. Companions, this exalted degree is the climax of Freemasonry. It is intimately blended with all that we are taught to desire and revere, both in this life and in that which is to come; our temporal and eternal affairs being so awfully and minutely interwoven. In all its disquisitions it has virtue for its aim, and the glory of God for its object, whilst the eternal welfare of mankind is considered in every point and letter of its ineffable mysteries.

There are in our Masonic rituals a certain number of statements which, on the surface, appear to be either inaccurate or impossible. Some of these can, however, be penetrated by careful thought, whilst others would seem to have no explanation.

It would be a grave error to be dogmatic since the extent to which symbology can be understood depends entirely upon the advancement and capabilities of the individual. On the other hand, it would seem invidious to continually repeat statements that appear inaccurate without some attempt to understand them.

It does not lie within the compass of this paper to comment on all anomalies. If, Companions, it has given you some food for thought and a desire to further your Masonic knowledge, I shall feel most honoured to have presented it.

Exaltation into the Holy Royal Arch is not only an extremely interesting and beautiful ceremony, but it is also full of silent lessons to every Companion who witnesses it. The Craft is often referred to by Masons as the material side of Freemasonry, and the Royal Arch as the spiritual side, but our initiations into the Craft might well be likened to the "Reformation of a man", and the subsequent ceremony of Exaltation into the Holy Royal Arch to the "Regeneration of a Mason".

Finally, Companions, be all of one mind. Live in peace. And may the God of love and peace delight to dwell among you and bless you all for evermore.

CHAPTER 9
Symbols in the Holy Royal Arch

Exaltation into the Holy Royal Arch is not only a most interesting and beautiful ceremony but is also filled with silent lessons for every candidate who witnesses it. The Craft is often referred to by Masons as the material side of Freemasonry, the Holy Royal Arch as the spiritual side. Initiation in the Craft might well be likened to the 'Reformation of Man'. His subsequent Ceremony of Exaltation into the Holy Royal Arch as the 'Regeneration of a Mason.'

Masonry has to be lived before it can be fully understood – the form has to give way to the spirit. The deeper meaning of this dramatic ceremonial must be applied to the daily life of each of us. There is a hidden significance underlying our ritual it is not all on the surface. Some of us have not ascended to as high an intellectual level as others and others almost deny that there is a hidden significance. To them, Freemasonry meant that they should be happy and communicate happiness to others – little or nothing more than that. What then is the hidden side of Masonry? What is the true purpose of our system?

Masonry is a quest of the individual Mason's soul for the Divinity resident in his own heart. That is the general principle on which our whole system is based. All our ceremonies, our symbols and so on, come together to explain and elaborate this formula.

I am sure that our illustrious founders had this formula in mind whilst they searched the archives for ritual worthy of the Ceremony. A Royal Arch Temple is, or ought to be, sacred to every Freemason and the remembrance of what takes place within its closely guarded portals that safe retreat of peace and friendship ought not to be allowed to sink into oblivion. There is no doubt that our Companions of yesteryear have left us with a wealth of ritual, literature and legend for which we should be grateful and proud of such inheritance.

There are still amongst us those who care about preserving our beautiful ritual. There are some of us who still strive to try to emulate our illustrious predecessors. Why not all of us, Companions? The Mason who is too busy to read Masonic publications ought to have been too busy to join the Order. It may be said that there is something in us that can be without us, will be after us, and was before us. Though we cannot tell how it entered us – this spirit of Masonry is vital – for without that spirit, Masonry falls flat.

The Royal Arch Ceremony, as we know it today in the English ritual, is an emasculated ceremony, the full benefits of the rite could only be obtained in Ireland, Scotland, the United States and Bristol where the most important portion of the ceremony, "The Passing the Veils", is still preserved. The oldest Royal Arch Chapter in this famous Province is Charity Chapter, founded in

1769. At one time it stood ninth in seniority amongst all the English Chapters. Subsequently, owing to the falling out of other Chapters, it actually ranked among the first four Chapters in the United Kingdom.

The Holy Royal Arch in Bristol has a special position, for it has not only one of the oldest Chapters under the 'Moderns' working in its midst, dating from 1769, but it has preserved the record of the 1758 Ceremony. These records are the earliest known in this country or indeed elsewhere, except in the USA, where they date back to 1753.

The symbols used in Royal Arch Masonry are of great antiquity, and one of them, the equilateral triangle, was used as a symbol in religious teaching some thousands of years ago, as a symbol of both heaven and the Trinity. The two interlaced triangles of the Star of David may well stand for the two 'elements' essential to life: fire and water. In the earliest known stages of the history of man, particularly among the Chinese, the earth was symbolised as a square; hence the expression 'the four corners of the earth' is a familiar one to all Bible students and which is reputed to be at least twelve thousand years old.

The triangle, however, has always been associated with the Deity. It is for this reason that in knowledgeable Lodges the flap of the EA's apron is always kept upright, signifying that in the First Degree the Divine Principle has not yet been assimilated by the material part of the Apprentice's nature. It is, I think, much to be regretted that this practice has ceased to be generally observed today. An apex of the triangle points to the East on the altar.

It has been stated that the symbol of the interlaced triangles, representing pairs of opposites – male and female, fire and water, light and darkness was the cosmic design used in the land of Mu, some thirty-five thousand years ago. Modern Freemasonry, particularly the Ritual of the Holy Royal Arch, contains many fragments of the earliest known religious teachings of mankind. On the wall of an Egyptian temple, in large hieroglyphs, is the title or name under which the Deity was worshipped: *I Am that I Am*, the title by which Moses was bidden to reveal God to the Children of Israel in their Egyptian bondage. It is of further interest to note that the triple attributes of the endless immortality of the eternal, the *I Am that I Am* of Mosaical times, are found first in the old Egyptian ritual, the *Book of the Dead*, which dates from 4266 BC. The words are: 'I am Yesterday, Today and Tomorrow.'

When we refer to the number seven, our thoughts as Royal Arch Masons must instinctively turn to the steps by which every Exaltee approaches the altar at the centre, on which the Ineffable Name is displayed. Seven was the Hebrew holy number and the Creator is said to have rested on the seventh day. This number is invariably mentioned in the VSL in connection with holy things. In Jewish festivals, we have mention of seven bullocks and seven rams; in the *Book of Joshua* seven priests bore seven trumpets; the Creation is said to have been completed in seven days, or seven epochs. After feeding the five thousand on the shores of Lake Galilee, seven loaves and seven baskets full of fragments were gathered up. The Virgin is crowned with seven stars as is the sun on the First Degree Tracing Board, whilst Mary Magdalene was afflicted by seven devils. We have also the Seven Liberal Arts and Sciences. There were the seven lamps of the Temple and, in the New Testament, there were seven wise Virgins and seven foolish ones. In Egyptian mythology also the 'ladder' of seven staves or rungs was connected with the most profound mysteries. This number has also been regarded as representative of self-sacrifice and of all the higher virtues.

In the Exaltation Ceremony according to the Bristol Rite, the candidate has to make seven circumambulations up and down the Chapter. This number, as well as being the "number of perfection", may also be considered to be typical of the seventy years' journeying in the wilderness.

Again, in practically every religious system, the number three is regarded as a sacred number. In ancient Egypt, the Triune was worshipped as a Trinity of Father, Mother and Child. The Druids venerated the three-leafed shamrock and Saint Patrick is said to have used it to teach the doctrine of the Trinity. It occurs in Buddhism, his word is his Church, while his followers are instructed how to attain the three Virtues – of Endurance, Courage and Obedience to the Law. In the Middle Ages, the triangle was regarded as the symbol of the Logos, which may be considered to be representative of the Creative Word, the in-dwelling reason and reasoned thought. It occurs in Christianity, though it is purely male in Father, Son and Holy Ghost.

The triangle of the Egyptian Trinity is also remarkable from another guise. Taking the 3-4-5 or right-angled triangle we have: three, representing Osiris; four, Isis the Great Earth-Mother; whilst the hypotenuse, five, the result of the conjunction of three and four at a particular angle, gives us the Child, Horus. It is from this that the popular opinion existing down to the present day that even numbers are supposed to be unlucky and odd numbers – lucky, has arisen. As you will see, in the Egyptian triangle, the odd numbers were male three and five, Osiris and Horus the only even number, four, was associated with the female or inferior member of the Triad, Isis. Hence the ancient Masonic question and answer: 'Why do all odds make a Lodge?' The answer is; 'Because all odds are to man's advantage.'

We are told that the mysterious Tau is derived from the Hebrew, that it was in ancient times regarded as a mark or sign of life, that it was the brand of innocence, and that Ezekiel was commanded by the Almighty to place the mark or sign of the Tau on the forehead of the righteous man in Jerusalem to distinguish him from the idolatrous one. The word 'Tau' is synonymous with the Greek Tau, the name of the letter 'T' in the Greek alphabet. The Greeks obtained it from the Semites. In the Phoenician, Hebrew, and other Semitic alphabets, the name was Tau. As in Greek, so it was also in these languages. The Tau was the last letter of the alphabet, and just as now we speak of the 'Alpha and the Omega', so, in the Middle Ages, they spoke of the 'Alpha and the Tau'. In the passage of time, this letter has changed its name less than any other. Compare the present 'T' with those which were the corresponding signs in Phoenician and other Semitic languages. See that in all these forms it is in the shape of a cross. There are all kinds of crosses: St Andrew's; S. George's; Maltese cross (which the Post Office, in the early 1840s, used for cancelling postage stamps); and the different crosses used in heraldry are legion. The Tau, variously known as the St Anthony's Cross, the Phoenician Cross, and the Egyptian Cross, has been described as the 'commonest of all primitive symbols' and it is right in describing it as a sacred symbol, or symbol of life. Thus, Wilkinson, in his work on Egypt at the time of the Pharaohs, says: 'The Gods hold in one hand the sacred Tau, or "sign of life"', and in the fifteenth century poem by Lyng we read: 'This Banner is most mighty of Virtue, Most Noble sign and token of Tau.'

The Phoenicians invariably used it as part of their marks for branding cattle to prove ownership. In Europe, the Tau continued to be used for branding and stamping until quite recent times. Thus, in a 17th-century work by Astry we read: 'It is by the Tau they are stamped; with that they are assured of their real value.'

The Hebrew word for mark or sign is *Tav-Tau* and comes from the verb *tavey* to mark; and is used in the original Hebrew for the passage from Ezekiel, 'Go through the midst of the City, through the midst of Jerusalem, and set a mark on the foreheads of men'. The word for 'mark' which is used is *Tav*. Peculiarly enough, the word in that form occurs in the Old Testament only twice, the other being in the *Book of Job, 31:35*, which reads: 'Behold, my desire is that the Almighty would answer me and that mine adversary had written a book.'

Before the Sojourners were sent to investigate the site for the foundations they were told that they would be supplied with the necessary Working Implements. It is evident that there must have been a stock of such articles handy. It is wrong to say that digging has nothing to do with Masonry, because craftsmen, in bygone days, dug foundations as well as felling trees in the forests of Lebanon for the Temple. The crowbar is referred to as an 'Emblem of Uprightness'.

In much the same way a flagstaff pointing to the skies has been described. Originally, the colours of an army were attached to a spear; so to carry a spear horizontally, whilst on the march, was to endanger the lives of one's comrades. In the 16th century, the *corbeau*, or crow-iron with a beak, was used in sieges to catch, like a grapnel, the rocks of castle walls, in order to scale the works of the enemy. On the march, such crows were also held upright, so the crow was then regarded as much a symbol of rectitude as the flagstaff is today; and the plumb-line is mentioned in the *Extended Board of Installed Masters*. In the siege of Syracuse, Archimedes used the corbeau to drag defenders off the ramparts, and, if they fell safely to earth, they were made prisoners. So the crowbar, as an effective instrument, has a long and venerable history.

The twenty-four-inch gauge was an Egyptian device used for measuring, and it was also an emblem of the day, divided into three parts for Labour, Refreshment and Reflection, and Sleep. The square originated in Egypt, its form being suggested by the division of the circle into four equal parts, by lines drawn at right angles to each other. It was the Egyptian land-measure and became an emblem of Justice because, by its aid, the boundaries of land in dispute were officially Adjusted. The compasses probably originated in China over four thousand years ago. I am told that one of the oldest words in the many different Chinese languages is literally 'Square and Compasses'.

If we regard the allusion to our symbols and tools in the proper light instead of being quite out of place as some of our destructive critics allege they are, they form a really beautiful allegory. It is important to remember that it is by diligent spadework in this life that we make ourselves fit for the next. Whilst we thus ourselves dispose of our earthly remains, the dead bury their dead and as soon as our spiritual selves are released from their bodily restraint, we are taught to believe they ascend to the Grand Chapter Above.

LAUGHTER
on the
LEVEL

Martin Faulks

- Are you ready for a sponsored laugh? Do you believe that Freemasonry should be fun? If so then this is the book for you. *Laughter on the Level* is a handy compendium of Masonic jokes and one-liners, that fits easily into your pocket. Unlike other joke books designed for use at the festive board, this title contains jokes only about Freemasons and Freemasonry. If you don't know how many Freemasons it takes to change a lightbulb, or the one about the Masonic parrot, then you are just going to have to buy the book!

- All royalties from the sale of this book are donated to Break, a charity that provides holidays and respite care for children and adults with learning disabilities from all areas of the country. Help bring relief to those suffering from hard challenges in life.

- Perhaps laughter is the best medicine after all!

Paperback • £9.99

Lewis Masonic • Riverdene Business Park
Molesey Road • Hersham • Surrey KT12 4RG
Tel: 01932 266635
Fax: 01932 266636
Email: vera.west@lewismasonic.co.uk

Visit us online at: www.lewismasonic.com